The Giver of Hope

Copyright © 2022 Lee Fredrickson
Published by 21st Century Press
Springfield, MO 65807

21st Century Press is a Christian publisher dedicated to publishing books that have a high standard of family values. We believe the vision for our company is to provide families and individuals with user-friendly materials that will help them in their daily lives and experiences. It is our prayer that this book will help you discover Biblical truth for your own life and help you meet the needs of others. May God richly bless you.

21st Century Press
2131 W. Republic Rd, MB 211
Springfield MO 65807
email: lee@21stcenturypress.com

ISBN: TP 978-1-951774-31-8
ISBN: eBook 978-1-951774-32-5

Editor: Lee Fredrickson
Visual and Learning Strategist: Monty Maple
Cover Design: Keith Locke Web: www.SeekFirst.org
Cover Illustration: Mark Fredrickson
Visit our website at: www.21stcenturypress.com
Visit I Am Jesus website: www.iamjesus.com
Printed in the United States of America

Navigating life's storms

One of the fascinating stories in this book relates to the moment when Jesus invited Peter to participate in a life-changing miraculous event.

The narrative continues from the story of Jesus feeding a multitude of 5,000 hungry men, women, and children with just a few loaves of bread and fish, with an abundance of leftovers. After this remarkable event, Jesus sent His disciples on a boat ahead of Him to cross the Sea of Galilee while He dismissed the crowd and went up a mountain to pray.

As night fell, a fierce storm erupted, causing the waves to become tumultuous and the winds to blow strongly. As dawn approached, Jesus decided to walk on the water to reach His disciples. At first, the disciples were terrified, mistaking Jesus for a ghost. But Jesus, knowing their fear, comforted them by saying, "Take courage. I am here!" Everyone was amazed, except Peter, who asked Jesus to command him to come out and walk on the water.

Jesus replied, "Yes, come." Peter stepped out of the boat and began walking towards Jesus. As long as Peter kept his gaze fixed on Jesus, he could walk on the water, despite the storm raging around him. Peter's faith in following Jesus out onto the water was truly remarkable. He did not act on his own accord but requested Jesus to command him to come.

This is the central theme of this book. Through the stories of Jesus, you will learn how to stop relying on the world or yourself as the source of truth and hope. Instead, you will learn to reach up to Jesus, the God who created you for a purpose for good, to navigate life's storms.

Contents

1. Jesus Came to the Earth He Created to Give Hope 13

2. The Mission of Hope Begins 23

3. The Message of Jesus Brings Hope to Everyone 27

4. The Power of Jesus Gives Hope 33

5. Because Jesus is God, He Can Deliver Hope 41

6. Jesus Gives Hope to the Hungry 47

7. Jesus is Our Source of Hope 57

8. Jesus Knows Your Needs Before You Do 63

9. The Power of Healing Leads to Hope 69

10. Jesus is the Door to Hope 73

11. Jesus Can Raise You to New Life 79

12. Many Believe the Message of Hope 83

13. The Humility of Jesus Shows Hope 89

14. The Promise of Jesus Seals the Hope in Us 93

15. The Hope Living in You Brings Joy 97

16. The Presence of Jesus in You is Your Hope 99

17. The Prayer of Jesus For You Gives You Hope 103

18. Jesus Died For You 107

19. The Preparation For Our Hope 111

20. Jesus Will Empty Your Tomb 119

21. Jesus Appeared on the Lake Shore 127

22. Jesus is in the Best Place to Help You 131

23. Do You Know That You Will Live Forever With Jesus in Heaven? 132

Jesus

You live in a world where trust is hard, love is temporary, and life seems so difficult. If you are like most people, you often wonder if there is something more to life. You want to trust and have stability in your life. You want to experience lasting love and be loved. You want to be able to provide for those you love and care for. The answer has always been there in Jesus, the One who created you, to trust, love, and walk with you through life's ups and downs.

SCAN ME

#TrustJesus

Trust

You put your trust in something every day.

Are you looking for something you can rely on?

Trust in Jesus with all your heart; do not depend on your own understanding.

Love

Jesus designed you
to love and be loved.

Are you satisfied ?

For God so loved the world that He gave His only begotten
Son, that whoever believes in Him should not perish but
have everlasting life. For God did not send His Son into the
world to condemn the world, but that the world through
Him might be saved.

SCAN ME

8

love

#loveJesus

Walk

Jesus created you with a purpose for good.

Are you pursuing a path that is meaningful?

Watch the path of your feet And all your ways will be established. Let Jesus be your guide through life.

SCAN ME

#WalkWithJesus

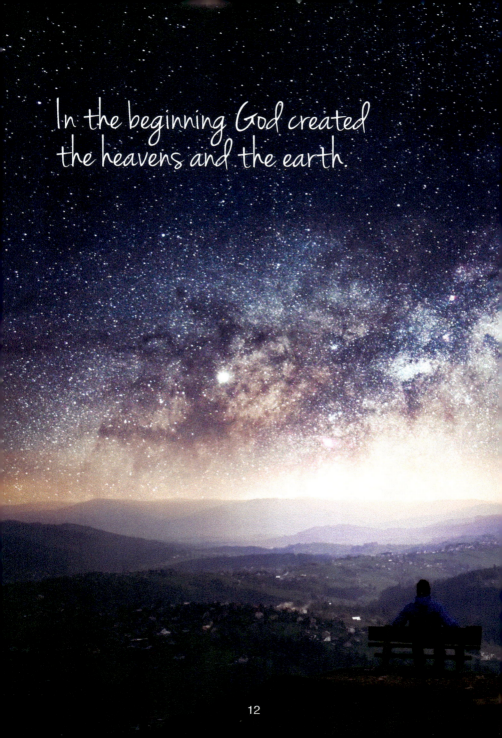

In the beginning God created
the heavens and the earth.

1

Jesus Came to the Earth He Created to Give Hope

The origin of Jesus was not as an ordinary human. He had no beginning and He has no ending. He is God. With the message of John the Baptist concerning Jesus, the evidence begins to build in this Gospel that Jesus, and Jesus alone, is the hope of the world, the hope of every individual.

He Created You for a Purpose - John 1:1-5

In the beginning the Word already existed. The Word was with God, and the Word was God. He existed in the beginning with God. God created everything through him, and nothing was created except through him. The Word gave life to everything that was created, and his life brought light to everyone. The light shines in the darkness, and the darkness can never extinguish it.

#WalkWithJesus.—If you are like most people, you want to live a life that matters. You want to know the purpose for which you were created, that will bring joy to your family and friends and give meaning to life. The good news is - you can! This book is a blueprint that reveals Jesus' purpose for you and reveals your destiny designed by His Father to accomplish His will in your life and the life of all believers. Even more importantly, you will enjoy the peace that only comes from a relationship with God through Jesus.

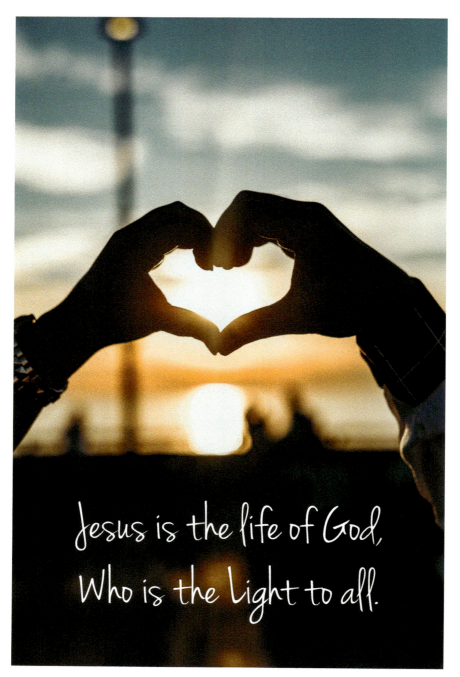

Jesus is the life of God,
Who is the Light to all.

John's Witness of the Hope - John 1:6-18

God sent a man, John the Baptist, to tell about the light so that everyone might believe because of his testimony. John himself was not the light; he was simply a witness to tell about the light. The one who is the true light, who gives light to everyone, was coming into the world.

He came into the very world he created, but the world didn't recognize him. He came to his own people, and even they rejected him. But to all who believed him and accepted him, he gave the right to become children of God. They are reborn—not with a physical birth resulting from human passion or plan, but a birth that comes from God.

So the Word became human and made his home among us. He was full of unfailing love and faithfulness. And we have seen his glory, the glory of the Father's one and only Son.

John testified about him when he shouted to the crowds, "This is the one I was talking about when I said, 'Someone is coming after me who is far greater than I am, for he existed long before me.'"

From his abundance we have all received one gracious blessing after another. For the law was given through Moses, but God's unfailing love and faithfulness came through Jesus Christ. No one has ever seen God. But the unique One, who is himself God, is near to the Father's heart. He has revealed God to us.

#LoveJesus.—"Let this mind be in you which was also in Christ Jesus, who, being in the form of God, did not consider it robbery to be equal with God, but made Himself of no reputation, taking the form of a bondservant, and coming in the likeness of men. And being found in appearance as a man, He humbled Himself and became obedient to the point of death, even the death of the cross."

16

John Was Not the Hope of the World
- John 1:19-28

This was John's testimony when the Jewish leaders sent priests and Temple assistants from Jerusalem to ask John, "Who are you?" He came right out and said, "I am not the Messiah."

"Well then, who are you?" they asked. "Are you Elijah?"

"No," he replied.

"Are you the Prophet we are expecting?"

"No."

"Then who are you? We need an answer for those who sent us. What do you have to say about yourself?"

John replied in the words of the prophet Isaiah:

"I am a voice shouting in the wilderness,

'Clear the way for the Lord's coming!'"

Then the Pharisees who had been sent asked him, "If you aren't the Messiah or Elijah or the Prophet, what right do you have to baptize?"

John told them, "I baptize with water, but right here in the crowd is someone you do not recognize. Though his ministry follows mine, I'm not even worthy to be his slave and untie the straps of his sandal."

This encounter took place in Bethany, an area east of the Jordan River, where John was baptizing.

#WalkWithJesus.—When Jesus does a great work in your heart, it is hard to keep quiet. Just as a light must shine, you will want to tell others what He has done for you. Will you tell someone today?

Jesus' Baptism Began His Ministry of Hope For You
- John 1:29-34

The next day John saw Jesus coming toward him, and said, "Behold! The Lamb of God who takes away the sin of the world! This is He of whom I said, 'After me comes a Man who is preferred before me, for He was before me.' I did not know Him; but that He should be revealed to Israel, therefore I came baptizing with water."

And John bore witness, saying, "I saw the Spirit descending from heaven like a dove, and He remained upon Him. I did not know Him, but He who sent me to baptize with water said to me, 'Upon whom you see the Spirit descending, and remaining on Him, this is He who baptizes with the Holy Spirit.' And I have seen and testified that this is the Son of God."

#WalkWithJesus.—Will you follow Jesus wherever He leads? He will give you a willing spirit, courage to endure, and strength to do it.

#YourTurn.—Jesus, I will follow wherever you lead me. Give me a willing spirit, the courage to endure, and a reliance on your strength to do it.

Jesus Met Six Disciples - John 1:35-51

The following day John was again standing with two of his disciples. As Jesus walked by, John looked at him and declared, "Look! There is the Lamb of God!" When John's two disciples heard this, they followed Jesus.

Jesus looked around and saw them following. "What do you want?" he asked them.

They replied, "Rabbi" (which means "Teacher"), "where are you staying?"

"Come and see," he said. It was about four o'clock in the afternoon when they went with him to the place where he was staying, and they remained with him the rest of the day.

Andrew, Simon Peter's brother, was one of these men who heard what John said and then followed Jesus. Andrew went to find his brother, Simon, and told him, "We have found the Messiah" (which means "Christ").

Then Andrew brought Simon to meet Jesus. Looking intently at Simon, Jesus said, "Your name is Simon, son of John—but you will be called Cephas" (which means "Peter").

The next day Jesus decided to go to Galilee. He found Philip and said to him, "Come, follow me." Philip was from Bethsaida, Andrew and Peter's hometown.

Philip went to look for Nathanael and told him, "We have found the very person Moses and the prophets wrote about! His name is Jesus, the son of Joseph from Nazareth."

"Nazareth!" exclaimed Nathanael. "Can anything good come from Nazareth?"

"Come and see for yourself," Philip replied.

As they approached, Jesus said, "Now here is a genuine son of Israel—a man of complete integrity."

"How do you know about me?" Nathanael asked.

Jesus replied, "I could see you under the fig tree before Philip found you."

Then Nathanael exclaimed, "Rabbi, you are the Son of God—the King of Israel!"

Jesus asked him, "Do you believe this just because I told you I had seen you under the fig tree? You will see greater things than this." Then he said, "I tell you the truth, you will all see heaven open and the angels of God going up and down on the Son of Man, the one who is the stairway between heaven and earth."

#WalkWithJesus.—Tell your family and friends about Jesus, and bring them to know Him as their Lord and Savior? You can find answers to all of your questions in Jesus. Focus your sight on Him, and see the greatness of His character, the beauty of His love, His compassion for those who are hurting, His forgiveness for all sin, His friendship to the friendless, His joy that comes from seeing the happiness and the harmony of those who believe in Him.

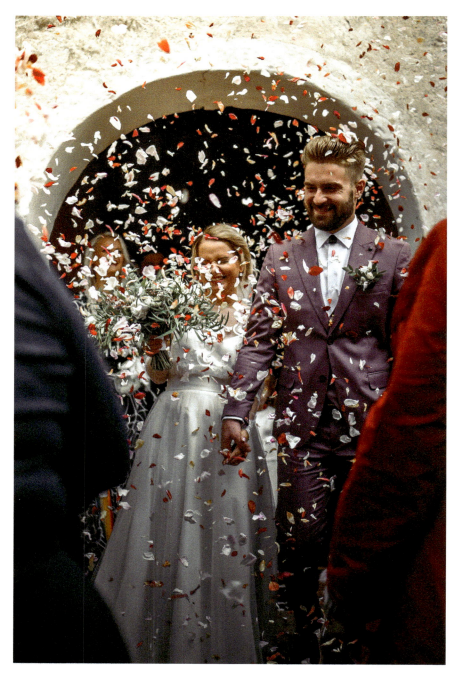

2

The Mission of Hope Begins

It is not surprising that the ministry of Hope to the world is first shown to us through a request at a simple wedding. The ministry of Hope is a ministry to the basic needs of every person. You have personal needs, and you have needs known only to you and God the Father. The greatest need is salvation in His Son Jesus.

Jesus Performed a Miracle at a Wedding Ceremony - John 2:1-12

The next day there was a wedding celebration in the village of Cana in Galilee. Jesus' mother was there, and Jesus and his disciples were also invited to the celebration. The wine supply ran out during the festivities, so Jesus' mother told him, "They have no more wine."

"Dear woman, that's not our problem," Jesus replied. "My time has not yet come."

But his mother told the servants, "Do whatever he tells you."

Standing nearby were six stone water jars, used for Jewish ceremonial washing. Each could hold twenty to thirty gallons. Jesus told the servants, "Fill the jars with water." When the jars had been filled, he said, "Now dip some out, and take it to the master of ceremonies." So the servants followed his instructions.

When the master of ceremonies tasted the water that was now wine, not knowing where it had come from (though, of course, the servants knew), he called the bridegroom over. "A host always serves the best wine first," he said. "Then, when everyone has had a lot to drink, he brings out the less expensive wine. But you have kept the best until now!"

water to wine
by Monty Maple

This miraculous sign at Cana in Galilee was the first time Jesus revealed his glory. And his disciples believed in him.

After the wedding he went to Capernaum for a few days with his mother, his brothers, and his disciples.

#WalkWithJesus.—This was the first sign miracle of Jesus, the creator of the universe, and proves Jesus is still Master of Creation, having the power to alter substance, when He turned the water to wine.

Jesus Cleansed the Temple. He Can Cleanse You
- John 2:13-23

It was nearly time for the Jewish Passover celebration, so Jesus went to Jerusalem. In the Temple area he saw merchants selling cattle, sheep, and doves for sacrifices; he also saw dealers at tables exchanging foreign money. Jesus made a whip from some ropes and chased them all out of the Temple. He drove out the sheep and cattle, scattered the money changers' coins over the floor, and turned over their tables. Then, going over to the people who sold doves, he told them, "Get these things out of here. Stop turning my Father's house into a marketplace!"

Then his disciples remembered this prophecy from the Scriptures: "Passion for God's house will consume me."

But the Jewish leaders demanded, "What are you doing? If God gave you authority to do this, show us a miraculous sign to prove it."

"All right," Jesus replied. "Destroy this temple, and in three days I will raise it up."

"What!" they exclaimed. "It has taken forty-six years to build this Temple, and you can rebuild it in three days?" But when Jesus said "this temple," he meant his own body. After he was raised from the dead, his disciples remembered he had said this, and they believed both the Scriptures and what Jesus had said.

Because of the miraculous signs Jesus did in Jerusalem at the Passover celebration, many began to trust in him. But Jesus didn't trust them, because he knew all about people. No one needed to tell him about human nature, for he knew what was in each person's heart.

#TrustJesus.—Jesus knows what is in your heart. He knows how hard it is for you to place your trust in someone. He is not like anyone you have ever met. He is God. Will you Trust Him?

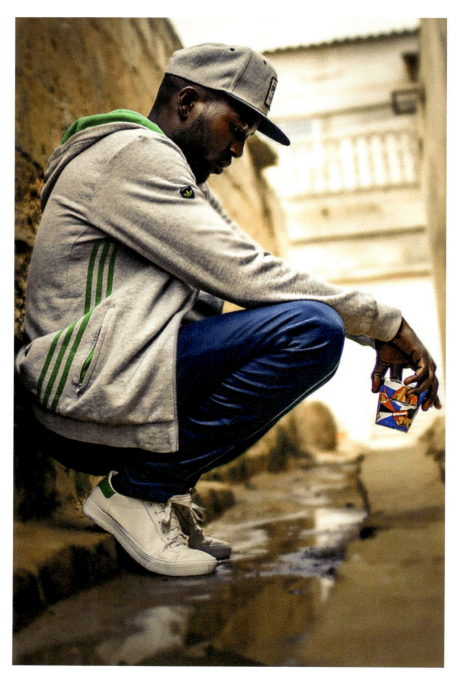

26

3

The Message of Jesus Brings Hope to Everyone

The ministry of the Lord Jesus Christ is not to one group of people, but to all of humankind, the up-and-out as well as the down-and-out of society. The need of every person is best met when the Lord Jesus Christ has the prominent place in the life of that individual.

You Must be Born Again to See Heaven - John 3:1-21

There was a man named Nicodemus, a Jewish religious leader who was a Pharisee. After dark one evening, he came to speak with Jesus. "Rabbi," he said, "we all know that God has sent you to teach us. Your miraculous signs are evidence that God is with you."

Jesus replied, "I tell you the truth, unless you are born again, you cannot see the Kingdom of God."

"What do you mean?" exclaimed Nicodemus. "How can an old man go back into his mother's womb and be born again?"

Jesus replied, "I assure you, no one can enter the Kingdom of God without being born of water and the Spirit. Humans can reproduce only human life, but the Holy Spirit gives birth to spiritual life. So don't be surprised when I say, 'You must be born again.' The wind blows wherever it wants. Just as you can hear the wind but can't tell where it comes from or where it is going, so you can't explain how people are born of the Spirit."

"How are these things possible?" Nicodemus asked.

Jesus replied, "You are a respected Jewish teacher, and yet you don't understand these things? I assure you, we tell you what we know and have seen, and yet you won't believe our testimony. But if you don't believe me when I tell you about earthly things, how can you possibly believe if I tell you about heavenly things? No one has ever gone to heaven and returned. But the Son of Man has come down from heaven. And as Moses lifted up the bronze snake on a pole in the wilderness, so the Son of Man must be lifted up, so that everyone who believes in him will have eternal life.

"For this is how God loved the world: He gave his one and only Son, so that everyone who believes in him will not perish but have eternal life. God sent his Son into the world not to judge the world, but to save the world through him.

"There is no judgment against anyone who believes in him. But anyone who does not believe in him has already been judged for not believing in God's one and only Son. And the judgment is based on this fact: God's light came into the world, but people loved the darkness more than the light, for their actions were evil. All who do evil hate the light and refuse to go near it for fear their sins will be exposed. But those who do what is right come to the light so others can see that they are doing what God wants."

#LoveJesus.—God loves you so much that He graciously did not spare Jesus, but allowed Jesus to die to save you from an eternity separated from Him. Nothing in this world will succeed against you. It is as sure as the certainty that God loves you. Jesus wants you to know that you can have this eternal life, "You must be born again." Will you place your complete trust in Jesus today?

#YourTurn.—Jesus, I am making a decision to place my complete trust in you for eternal life in heaven.

نهر الأردن
Jordan River

Jesus is the Only Hope for Humankind - John 3:22-36

Then Jesus and his disciples left Jerusalem and went into the Judean countryside. Jesus spent some time with them there, baptizing people.

At this time John the Baptist was baptizing at Aenon, near Salim, because there was plenty of water there; and people kept coming to him for baptism. (This was before John was thrown into prison.) A debate broke out between John's disciples and a certain Jew over ceremonial cleansing. So John's disciples came to him and said, "Rabbi, the man you met on the other side of the Jordan River, the one you identified as the Messiah, is also baptizing people. And everybody is going to him instead of coming to us."

John replied, "No one can receive anything unless God gives it from heaven. You yourselves know how plainly I told you, 'I am not the Messiah. I am only here to prepare the way for him.' It is the bridegroom who marries the bride, and the bridegroom's friend is simply glad to stand with him and hear his vows. Therefore, I am filled with joy at his success. He must become greater and greater, and I must become less and less.

"He has come from above and is greater than anyone else. We are of the earth, and we speak of earthly things, but he has come from heaven and is greater than anyone else. He testifies about what he has seen and heard, but how few believe what he tells them! Anyone who accepts his testimony can affirm that God is true. For he is sent by God. He speaks God's words, for God gives him the Spirit without limit. The Father loves his Son and has put everything into his hands. And anyone who believes in God's Son has eternal life. Anyone who doesn't obey the Son will never experience eternal life but remains under God's angry judgment.

#LoveJesus.—Jesus is humankind's only hope for eternal life. He breathes new life in all who would put their complete trust in Him. Hope in the here and now and hope for eternity rests on the shoulders of Jesus, who is for you today the Way, the Truth, and the Life. How's that for hope?

Anyone who drinks this water will soon become thirsty again. But those who drink the water I give will never be thirsty again. It becomes a fresh, bubbling spring within them, giving them eternal life.

—Jesus

4

The Power of Jesus Gives Hope

The extent of the hope found in the Lord Jesus Christ reaches to those who are looked down on by others. The Lord Jesus Christ is not willing that anyone should perish but every person, no matter their status, should receive the hope of eternal life with Him.

A Life Changed Forever - John 4:1-42

Jesus knew the Pharisees had heard that he was baptizing and making more disciples than John (though Jesus himself didn't baptize them—his disciples did). So he left Judea and returned to Galilee.

He had to go through Samaria on the way. Eventually he came to the Samaritan village of Sychar, near the field that Jacob gave to his son Joseph. Jacob's well was there; and Jesus, tired from the long walk, sat wearily beside the well about noontime. Soon a Samaritan woman came to draw water, and Jesus said to her, "Please give me a drink." He was alone at the time because his disciples had gone into the village to buy some food.

The woman was surprised, for Jews refuse to have anything to do with Samaritans. She said to Jesus, "You are a Jew, and I am a Samaritan woman. Why are you asking me for a drink?"

Jesus replied, "If you only knew the gift God has for you and who you are speaking to, you would ask me, and I would give you living water."

"But sir, you don't have a rope or a bucket," she said, "and this well is very deep. Where would you get this living water? And besides, do you think you're greater than our ancestor Jacob, who gave us this well? How can you offer better water than he and his sons and his animals enjoyed?"

Jesus replied, "Anyone who drinks this water will soon become thirsty again. But those who drink the water I give will never be thirsty again. It becomes a fresh, bubbling spring within them, giving them eternal life."

"Please, sir," the woman said, "give me this water! Then I'll never be thirsty again, and I won't have to come here to get water."

"Go and get your husband," Jesus told her.

"I don't have a husband," the woman replied.

Jesus said, "You're right! You don't have a husband—for you have had five husbands, and you aren't even married to the man you're living with now. You certainly spoke the truth!"

"Sir," the woman said, "you must be a prophet. So tell me, why is it that you Jews insist that Jerusalem is the only place of worship, while we Samaritans claim it is here at Mount Gerizim, where our ancestors worshiped?"

Jesus replied, "Believe me, dear woman, the time is coming when it will no longer matter whether you worship the Father on this mountain or in Jerusalem. You Samaritans know very little about the one you worship, while we Jews know all about him, for salvation comes through the Jews. But the time is coming—indeed it's here now—when true worshipers will worship the Father in spirit and in truth. The Father is looking for those who will worship him that way. For God is Spirit, so those who worship him must worship in spirit and in truth."

The woman said, "I know the Messiah is coming—the one who is called Christ. When he comes, he will explain everything to us."

Then Jesus told her, "I Am the Messiah!"

Just then his disciples came back. They were shocked to find him talking to a woman, but none of them had the nerve to ask, "What do you want with her?" or "Why are you talking to her?" The woman left her water jar beside the well and ran back to the village, telling everyone, "Come and see a man who told me everything I ever did! Could he possibly be the Messiah?" So the people came streaming from the village to see him.

Meanwhile, the disciples were urging Jesus, "Rabbi, eat something."

But Jesus replied, "I have a kind of food you know nothing about."

"Did someone bring him food while we were gone?" the disciples asked each other.

Then Jesus explained: "My nourishment comes from doing the will of God, who sent me, and from finishing his work. You know the saying, 'Four months between planting and harvest.' But I say, wake up and look around. The fields are already ripe for harvest. The harvesters are paid good wages, and the fruit they harvest is people brought to eternal life. What joy awaits both the planter and the harvester alike! You know the saying, 'One plants and another harvests.' And it's true. I sent you to harvest where you didn't plant; others had already done the work, and now you will get to gather the harvest."

Many Samaritans from the village believed in Jesus because the woman had said, "He told me everything I ever did!" When they came out to see him, they begged him to stay in their village. So he stayed for two days, long enough for many more to hear his message and believe.

Then they said to the woman, "Now we believe, not just because of what you told us, but because we have heard him ourselves. Now we know that he is indeed the Savior of the world."

#TrustJesus.—Believing in Jesus is like eating and drinking from all that He is. It goes beyond what your soul thirsts for. He will satisfy you so that you will never thirst again. He is the end of your quest for satisfaction. When you trust Him the way God intends for you too, His presence in your life and His promises will be so satisfying that you will not be dominated by the alluring pleasures of sin. Faith in Jesus nullifies the power of sin in your life and enables obedience to Him alone. Will you place your complete faith in Jesus today?

#YourTurn.—Jesus, I've spent time and energy seeking the wrong way to satisfy my thirst in this world. I've learned that things and people can't satisfy, when I try to quench my thirst apart from you. I desire, more than anything, to drink and be satisfied with the water of life that only You can give. I want Your presence in my life and I hold tight to Your promise that You will never leave me. I place my complete faith in You.

Healing the Nobleman's Son Shows the Power of Hope - John 4:43-54

At the end of the two days, Jesus went on to Galilee. He himself had said that a prophet is not honored in his own hometown. Yet the Galileans welcomed him, for they had been in Jerusalem at the Passover celebration and had seen everything he did there.

As he traveled through Galilee, he came to Cana, where he had turned the water into wine. There was a government official in nearby Capernaum whose son was very sick. When he heard that Jesus had come from Judea to Galilee, he went and begged Jesus to come to Capernaum to heal his son, who was about to die.

Jesus asked, "Will you never believe in me unless you see miraculous signs and wonders?"

The official pleaded, "Lord, please come now before my little boy dies."

Then Jesus told him, "Go back home. Your son will live!" And the man believed what Jesus said and started home.

While the man was on his way, some of his servants met him with the news that his son was alive and well. He asked them when the boy had begun to get better, and they replied, "Yesterday afternoon at one o'clock his fever suddenly disappeared!" Then the father realized that that was the very time Jesus had told him, "Your son will live." And he and his entire household believed in Jesus. This was the second miraculous sign Jesus did in Galilee after coming from Judea.

#WalkWithJesus.—This second sign miracle proves Jesus is not limited by geography, having the power to heal from afar. All Jesus had to do was tell the man, "Go your way. Your son will live." This emphasizes that Jesus' word alone has power and reminds us that He is God, as John says: "the Word was with God and the Word was God."

Modern Day Capernaum

5

Because Jesus is God, He Can Deliver Hope

Most people are grasping for something to give them hope. You can be certain of the hope that is found only in the Lord Jesus Christ. So, "Rejoice in your confident hope. Be patient in trouble, and keep on praying."

A Visit to A Pool - John 5:1-9

Afterward Jesus returned to Jerusalem for one of the Jewish holy days. Inside the city, near the Sheep Gate, was the pool of Bethesda, with five covered porches. Crowds of sick people—blind, lame, or paralyzed—lay on the porches. One of the men lying there had been sick for thirty-eight years. When Jesus saw him and knew he had been ill for a long time, he asked him, "Would you like to get well?"

"I can't, sir," the sick man said, "for I have no one to put me into the pool when the water bubbles up. Someone else always gets there ahead of me."

Jesus told him, "Stand up, pick up your mat, and walk!"

Instantly, the man was healed! He rolled up his sleeping mat and began walking! But this miracle happened on the Sabbath.

#TrustJesus.—This third sign miracle proves Jesus is not limited by time; both because the miracle healed an infirmity of nearly four decades, and because it was performed on the Sabbath.

The Man Jesus Healed Went to the Temple - John 5:10-16

So, the Jewish leaders objected. They said to the man who was cured, "You can't work on the Sabbath! The law doesn't allow you to carry that sleeping mat!"

But he replied, "The man who healed me told me, 'Pick up your mat and walk.'"

"Who said such a thing as that?" they demanded.

The man didn't know, for Jesus had disappeared into the crowd. But afterward Jesus found him in the Temple and told him, "Now you are well; so stop sinning, or something even worse may happen to you." Then the man went and told the Jewish leaders that it was Jesus who had healed him.

So the Jewish leaders began harassing Jesus for breaking the Sabbath rules.

#TrustJesus.—Don't give up when testings come your way. Just trust that Jesus will never leave you nor forsake you, no matter how long you have been waiting. Trust Jesus today and accept Him as your personal Lord and Savior.

Jesus is Equal With God - John 5:17-23

But Jesus replied, "My Father is always working, and so am I." So the Jewish leaders tried all the harder to find a way to kill him. For he not only broke the Sabbath, he called God his Father, thereby making himself equal with God.

So Jesus explained, "I tell you the truth, the Son can do nothing by himself. He does only what he sees the Father doing. Whatever the Father does, the Son also does. For the Father loves the Son and shows him everything he is doing. In fact, the Father will show him how to do even greater works than healing this man. Then you will truly be astonished. For just as the Father gives life to those he raises from the dead, so the Son gives life to anyone he wants. In addition, the Father judges no one. Instead, he has given the Son absolute authority to judge, so that everyone will honor the Son, just as they honor the Father. Anyone who does not honor the Son is certainly not honoring the Father who sent him.

#TrustJesus.—Honor Jesus for who He really is—He is the divine Son of God, the Messiah, the crucified and risen Savior of the world, the Lord of the universe and Judge of all human beings? Believe His word today, and you will not come into judgment but you will pass from death to life. Jesus became all this for you when He died on the cross and rose the third day. This is the greatest news beyond all words. This is your confident hope of eternal life.

Now I See
by Monty Maple

Life and Judgment Are Through Jesus - John 5:24-30

"I tell you the truth, those who listen to my message and believe in God who sent me have eternal life. They will never be condemned for their sins, but they have already passed from death into life.

"And I assure you that the time is coming, indeed it's here now, when the dead will hear my voice—the voice of the Son of God. And those who listen will live. The Father has life in himself, and he has granted that same life-giving power to his Son. And he has given him authority to judge everyone because he is the Son of Man. Don't be so surprised! Indeed, the time is coming when all the dead in their graves will hear the voice of God's Son, and they will rise again. Those who have done good will rise to experience eternal life, and those who have continued in evil will rise to experience judgment. I can do nothing on my own. I judge as God tells me. Therefore, my judgment is just, because I carry out the will of the one who sent me, not my own will."

#TrustJesus.—The resurrection of life is the promise of God that everyone who trusts in Jesus will be the beneficiaries of His power to lead them down the right path in life, and one day to heaven. Will you believe in your heart that God raised Jesus from the dead, and trust, in your heart, that He will save you?

Jesus Has Four Witnesses to Prove That He is God
- John 5:31-47

John the Baptizer: "If I were to testify on my own behalf, my testimony would not be valid. But someone else is also testifying about me, and I assure you that everything he says about me is true. In fact, you sent investigators to listen to John the Baptist, and his testimony about me was true. Of course, I have no need of human witnesses, but I say these things so you might be saved. John was like a burning and shining lamp, and you were excited for a while about his message.

Jesus' Miracles: "But I have a greater witness than John—my teachings and my miracles. The Father gave me these works to accomplish, and they prove that he sent me.

God, The Father's, Voice: "And the Father who sent me has testified about me himself. You have never heard his voice or seen him face to face, and you do not have his message in your hearts, because you do not believe me—the one he sent to you.

The Scriptures: "You search the Scriptures because you think they give you eternal life. But the Scriptures point to me! Yet you refuse to come to me to receive this life.

"Your approval means nothing to me, because I know you don't have God's love within you. For I have come to you in my Father's name, and you have rejected me. Yet if others come in their own name, you gladly welcome them. No wonder you can't believe! For you gladly honor each other, but you don't care about the honor that comes from the one who alone is God.

"Yet it isn't I who will accuse you before the Father. Moses will accuse you! Yes, Moses, in whom you put your hopes. If you really believed Moses, you would believe me, because he wrote about me. But since you don't believe what he wrote, how will you believe what I say?"

#TrustJesus.—Search the Scriptures to know Jesus in salvation, and to grow in grace. He will open your spiritual eyes as you discover His presence concealed in the written Word.

Five Thousand Fed
by Monty Maple

SCAN ME

6

Jesus Gives Hope to the Hungry

The Lord Jesus Christ recognizes and desires to fulfill the needs of people that others might overlook. Although physical needs may be evident, spiritual needs hold greater importance in the context of eternity. Sin can cause individuals to overlook their most crucial needs, which are spiritual in nature. Despite this, the Lord Jesus Christ does not turn away from those who turn away from Him.

A Huge Crowd Followed Jesus - John 6:1-9

After this, Jesus crossed over to the far side of the Sea of Galilee, also known as the Sea of Tiberias. A huge crowd kept following him wherever he went, because they saw his miraculous signs as he healed the sick. Then Jesus climbed a hill and sat down with his disciples around him. (It was nearly time for the Jewish Passover celebration.) Jesus soon saw a huge crowd of people coming to look for him. Turning to Philip, he asked, "Where can we buy bread to feed all these people?" He was testing Philip, for he already knew what he was going to do.

Philip replied, "Even if we worked for months, we wouldn't have enough money to feed them!"

Then Andrew, Simon Peter's brother, spoke up. "There's a young boy here with five barley loaves and two fish. But what good is that with this huge crowd?"

#TrustJesus.—Jesus tested Phillip's faith by asking him how they could feed the people, even though Jesus already knew He was going to perform a miracle and feed them. Through this experience, Phillip learned the valuable lesson that true faith relies on God's resources, rather than physical or material ones. The other disciples also learned this lesson, which emphasizes that true saving faith recognizes that anything is possible with Jesus and that He will provide what is needed. This lesson teaches us that with Jesus, no situation is hopeless and that true faith requires trusting in His provision.

SCAN ME

48

Five-Thousand Were Fed - John 6:10-14

❚❚Tell everyone to sit down," Jesus said. So they all sat down on the grassy slopes. (The men alone numbered about 5,000.)

Then Jesus took the loaves, gave thanks to God, and distributed them to the people. Afterward he did the same with the fish. And they all ate as much as they wanted. After everyone was full, Jesus told his disciples, "Now gather the leftovers, so that nothing is wasted." So they picked up the pieces and filled twelve baskets with scraps left by the people who had eaten from the five barley loaves.

When the people saw him do this miraculous sign, they exclaimed, "Surely, he is the Prophet we have been expecting!"

When Jesus saw that they were ready to force him to be their king, he insisted that his disciples get back into the boat and cross to the other side of the lake, while he sent the people home. After sending them home, he went up into the hills by himself to pray. Night fell while he was there alone.

#TrustJesus.—This Fourth Sign miracle proves Jesus is the source of both physical needs, having the power to multiply a few loaves of bread and a few fish into enough food to feed over 5,000 and Spiritual needs, in that He is the Bread of Life. The purpose was clear. This miracle was performed so that you would believe and have eternal life. Will you trust Jesus as your Bread of Life?

Jesus Walked with Peter on the Water, He Will Walk With You Through Your Storm
- Matthew 14:24-36

Meanwhile, the disciples were in trouble far away from land, for a strong wind had risen, and they were fighting heavy waves. About three o'clock in the morning Jesus came toward them, walking on the water. When the disciples saw him walking on the water, they were terrified. In their fear, they cried out, "It's a ghost!"

But Jesus spoke to them at once. "Don't be afraid," he said. "Take courage. I am here!"

Then Peter called to him, "Lord, if it's really you, tell me to come to you, walking on the water."

"Yes, come," Jesus said.

So Peter went over the side of the boat and walked on the water toward Jesus. But when he saw the Strong wind and the waves, he was terrified and began to sink. "Save me, Lord!" he shouted.

Jesus immediately reached out and grabbed him. "You have so little faith," Jesus said. "Why did you doubt me?"

When they climbed back into the boat, the wind stopped. Then the disciples worshiped him. "You really are the Son of God!" they exclaimed.

After they had crossed the lake, they landed at Gennesaret. When the people recognized Jesus, the news of his arrival spread quickly throughout the whole area, and soon people were bringing all their sick to be healed. They begged him to let the sick touch at least the fringe of his robe, and all who touched him were healed.

#TrustJesus.—The fifth sign miracle performed by Jesus serves as evidence that He has authority over the natural world, transcending the limitations of physics. Jesus may permit storms in your life to challenge your faith, but He will also enable you to remain steadfast in your devotion to Him through every tempest you encounter. Follow the example of Peter and the disciples, who worshiped Jesus after He rescued them from the storm. Can you put your trust in Jesus amidst the highs and lows of life?

Jesus Will Give You a Different Kind of Bread
- John 6:22-41

The next day the crowd that had stayed on the far shore saw that the disciples had taken the only boat, and they realized Jesus had not gone with them. Several boats from Tiberias landed near the place where the Lord had blessed the bread and the people had eaten. So when the crowd saw that neither Jesus nor his disciples were there, they got into the boats and went across to Capernaum to look for him. They found him on the other side of the lake and asked, "Rabbi, when did you get here?"

Jesus replied, "I tell you the truth, you want to be with me because I fed you, not because you understood the miraculous signs. But don't be so concerned about perishable things like food. Spend your energy seeking the eternal life that the Son of Man can give you. For God the Father has given me the seal of his approval."

They replied, "We want to perform God's works, too. What should we do?"

Jesus told them, "This is the only work God wants from you: Believe in the one he has sent."

They answered, "Show us a miraculous sign if you want us to believe in you. What can you do? After all, our ancestors ate manna while they journeyed through the wilderness! The Scriptures say, 'Moses gave them bread from heaven to eat.'"

Jesus said, "I tell you the truth, Moses didn't give you bread from heaven. My Father did. And now he offers you the true bread from heaven. The true bread of God is the one who comes down from heaven and gives life to the world."

"Sir," they said, "give us that bread every day."

Jesus replied, "I am the bread of life. Whoever comes to me will never be hungry again. Whoever believes in me will never be thirsty. But you haven't believed in me even though you have seen me. However, those the Father has given me will come to me, and I will never reject them. For I have come down from heaven to do the will of God who sent me, not to do my own will. And this is the will of God, that I should not lose even one of all those he has given me, but that I should raise them up at the last day. For it is my Father's will that all who see his Son and believe in him should have eternal life. I will raise them up at the last day."

Then the people began to murmur in disagreement because he had said, "I am the bread that came down from heaven."

#TrustJesus.—Jesus is the Creator, God the Son, and He is the Bread of Life. He will fill you spiritually with the Bread of Life when you are weak.

Mahane Yehuda Market, Jerusalem, Israel

The Only Hope For the World is Rejected - John 6:42-59

They said, "Isn't this Jesus, the son of Joseph? We know his father and mother. How can he say, 'I came down from heaven'?"

But Jesus replied, "Stop complaining about what I said. For no one can come to me unless the Father who sent me draws them to me, and at the last day I will raise them up. As it is written in the Scriptures, 'They will all be taught by God.' Everyone who listens to the Father and learns from him comes to me. (Not that anyone has ever seen the Father; only I, who was sent from God, have seen him.)

"I tell you the truth, anyone who believes has eternal life. Yes, I am the bread of life! Your ancestors ate manna in the wilderness, but they all died. Anyone who eats the bread from heaven, however, will never die. I am the living bread that came down from heaven. Anyone who eats this bread will live forever; and this bread, which I will offer so the world may live, is my flesh."

Then the people began arguing with each other about what he meant. "How can this man give us his flesh to eat?" they asked.

So Jesus said again, "I tell you the truth, unless you eat the flesh of the Son of Man and drink his blood, you cannot have eternal life within you. But anyone who eats my flesh and drinks my blood has eternal life, and I will raise that person at the last day. For my flesh is true food, and my blood is true drink. Anyone who eats my flesh and drinks my blood remains in me, and I in him. I live because of the living Father who sent me; in the same way, anyone who feeds on me will live because of me. I am the true bread that came down from heaven. Anyone who eats this bread will not die as your ancestors did (even though they ate the manna) but will live forever."

He said these things while he was teaching in the synagogue in Capernaum.

#TrustJesus.—Will you place your complete faith and trust in Jesus as your Savior and Lord? He will satisfy your hunger and thirst to be made right in the sight of God. He is essential to life. Just accept Him today?

Many Disciples Turned Away From the Message of Hope - John 6:60-71

Many of his disciples said, "This is very hard to understand. How can anyone accept it?"

Jesus was aware that his disciples were complaining, so he said to them, "Does this offend you? Then what will you think if you see the Son of Man ascend to heaven again? The Spirit alone gives eternal life. Human effort accomplishes nothing. And the very words I have spoken to you are spirit and life. But some of you do not believe me." (For Jesus knew from the beginning which ones didn't believe, and he knew who would betray him.) Then he said, "That is why I said that people can't come to me unless the Father gives them to me."

At this point many of his disciples turned away and deserted him. Then Jesus turned to the Twelve and asked, "Are you also going to leave?"

Simon Peter replied, "Lord, to whom would we go? You have the words that give eternal life. We believe, and we know you are the Holy One of God."

Then Jesus said, "I chose the twelve of you, but one is a devil." He was speaking of Judas, son of Simon Iscariot, one of the Twelve, who would later betray him.

#TrustJesus.—Jesus' Father chose the disciples in love so they could be holy. He wants you to enter His presence to worship and praise Him. You can choose to live with Jesus forever in heaven according to His plan of salvation. He will accept you according to the good pleasure of His love. Will you accept Him today as your Lord and Savior?

Jesus is Our Source of Hope

The answers of life are not found in religion. The only place to find hope in this life and the life to come is in the person of the Lord Jesus Christ. Hope is centered in who He is.

Jesus' Brothers Did Not Believe in Him - John 7:1-9

After this, Jesus traveled around Galilee. He wanted to stay out of Judea, where the Jewish leaders were plotting his death. But soon it was time for the Jewish Festival of Shelters, and Jesus' brothers said to him, "Leave here and go to Judea, where your followers can see your miracles! You can't become famous if you hide like this! If you can do such wonderful things, show yourself to the world!" For even his brothers didn't believe in him.

Jesus replied, "Now is not the right time for me to go, but you can go anytime. The world can't hate you, but it does hate me because I accuse it of doing evil. You go on. I'm not going to this festival, because my time has not yet come." After saying these things, Jesus remained in Galilee.

> #TrustJesus.—In Jesus' life as well as our own, knowing the Father's will is just as important as knowing His timing. Because Jesus was completely submitted to the will of the Father, the timetable of God the Father was important. But for Jesus' brothers, who were not submitted to God's will in the same way, any time was fine! Many get discouraged because they sense they know God's will, but they move ahead of His timing.

Jesus Will Take Away All of Your Confusion
- John 7:10-36

But after his brothers left for the festival, Jesus also went, though secretly, staying out of public view. The Jewish leaders tried to find him at the festival and kept asking if anyone had seen him. There was a lot of grumbling about him among the crowds. Some argued, "He's a good man," but others said, "He's nothing but a fraud who deceives the people." But no one had the courage to speak favorably about him in public, for they were afraid of getting in trouble with the Jewish leaders.

Then, midway through the festival, Jesus went up to the Temple and began to teach. The people were surprised when they heard him. "How does he know so much when he hasn't been trained?" they asked.

So Jesus told them, "My message is not my own; it comes from God who sent me. Anyone who wants to do the will of God will know whether my teaching is from God or is merely my own. Those who speak for themselves want glory only for themselves, but a person who seeks to honor the one who sent him speaks truth, not lies. Moses gave you the law, but none of you obeys it! In fact, you are trying to kill me."

The crowd replied, "You're demon possessed! Who's trying to kill you?"

Jesus replied, "I did one miracle on the Sabbath, and you were amazed. But you work on the Sabbath, too, when you obey Moses' law of circumcision. (Actually, this tradition of circumcision began with the patriarchs, long before the law of Moses.) For if the correct time for circumcising your son falls on the Sabbath, you go ahead and do it so as not to break the law of Moses. So why should you be angry with me for healing a man on the Sabbath? Look beneath the surface so you can judge correctly."

Some of the people who lived in Jerusalem started to ask each other, "Isn't this the man they are trying to kill? But here he is, speaking in public, and they say nothing to him. Could our leaders possibly believe that he is the Messiah? But how could he be? For we know where this man comes from. When the Messiah comes, he will simply appear; no one will know where he comes from."

While Jesus was teaching in the Temple, he called out, "Yes, you know me, and you know where I come from. But I'm not here on my own. The one who sent me is true, and you don't know him. But I know him because I come from him, and he sent me to you." Then the leaders tried to arrest him; but no one laid a hand on him, because his time had not yet come.

Many among the crowds at the Temple believed in him. "After all," they said, "would you expect the Messiah to do more miraculous signs than this man has done?"

When the Pharisees heard that the crowds were whispering such things, they and the leading priests sent Temple guards to arrest Jesus. But Jesus told them, "I will be with you only a little longer. Then I will return to the one who sent me. You will search for me but not find me. And you cannot go where I am going."

The Jewish leaders were puzzled by this statement. "Where is he planning to go?" they asked. "Is he thinking of leaving the country and going to the Jews in other lands? Maybe he will even teach the Greeks! What does he mean when he says, 'You will search for me but not find me,' and 'You cannot go where I am going'?"

#TrustJesus.—Jesus is God. He knows the infinite past and He knows the infinite future. Will you live for Him today? Will you yield your future to Him? He will show you how to serve Him best.

Anyone Who is Thirsty May Come to Me
- John 7:37-53

On the last day, the climax of the festival, Jesus stood and shouted to the crowds, "Anyone who is thirsty may come to me! Anyone who believes in me may come and drink! For the Scriptures declare, 'Rivers of living water will flow from his heart.'" (When he said "living water," he was speaking of the Spirit, who would be given to everyone believing in him. But the Spirit had not yet been given, because Jesus had not yet entered into his glory.)

When the crowds heard him say this, some of them declared, "Surely this man is the Prophet we've been expecting." Others said, "He is the Messiah." Still others said, "But he can't be! Will the Messiah come from Galilee? For the Scriptures clearly state that the Messiah will be born of the royal line of David, in Bethlehem, the village where King David was born." So the crowd was divided about him. Some even wanted him arrested, but no one laid a hand on him.

When the Temple guards returned without having arrested Jesus, the leading priests and Pharisees demanded, "Why didn't you bring him in?"

"We have never heard anyone speak like this!" the guards responded.

"Have you been led astray, too?" the Pharisees mocked. "Is there a single one of us rulers or Pharisees who believes in him? This foolish crowd follows him, but they are ignorant of the law. God's curse is on them!"

Then Nicodemus, the leader who had met with Jesus earlier, spoke up. "Is it legal to convict a man before he is given a hearing?" he asked.

They replied, "Are you from Galilee, too? Search the Scriptures and see for yourself—no prophet ever comes from Galilee!"

Then the meeting broke up, and everybody went home.

#WalkWithJesus.—We invite you to come to Jesus. When you are weak, come to Jesus for strength to continue on. When you can't find happiness or satisfaction, come to Jesus to drink and to find purpose in life, and peace. He will fill you with His presence. Will you trust the future He has for you?

#YourTurn.—Jesus, I am making a decision to step out by faith and trust You. I know I am going to have questions, and I know you are going to be there with me. When I am weak, I know I can rely on your strength to continue on. When I can't find happiness and satisfaction in life, I know you will give me purpose in life and peace. I will trust you for the future you have for me.

8

Jesus Knows Your Needs Before You Do

I Am the Light of the World - John 8:1-11

Jesus returned to the Mount of Olives, but early the next morning he was back again at the Temple. A crowd soon gathered, and he sat down and taught them. As he was speaking, the teachers of religious law and the Pharisees brought a woman who had been caught in the act of adultery. They put her in front of the crowd.

"Teacher," they said to Jesus, "this woman was caught in the act of adultery. The law of Moses says to stone her. What do you say?"

They were trying to trap him into saying something they could use against him, but Jesus stooped down and wrote in the dust with his finger. They kept demanding an answer, so he stood up again and said, "All right, but let the one who has never sinned throw the first stone!" Then he stooped down again and wrote in the dust.

When the accusers heard this, they slipped away one by one, beginning with the oldest, until only Jesus was left in the middle of the crowd with the woman. Then Jesus stood up again and said to the woman, "Where are your accusers? Didn't even one of them condemn you?"

"No, Lord," she said.

And Jesus said, "Neither do I. Go and sin no more."

#WalkWithJesus.—Will you obey when Jesus enters your life? He will keep reminding you that no one is too hardened to follow Him as a dedicated disciple.

The Light Brings Hope to Those Living in Darkness
- John 8:12-20

Jesus spoke to the people once more and said, "I am the light of the world. If you follow me, you won't have to walk in darkness, because you will have the light that leads to life."

The Pharisees replied, "You are making those claims about yourself! Such testimony is not valid."

Jesus told them, "These claims are valid even though I make them about myself. For I know where I came from and where I am going, but you don't know this about me. You judge me by human standards, but I do not judge anyone. And if I did, my judgment would be correct in every respect because I am not alone. The Father who sent me is with me. Your own law says that if two people agree about something, their witness is accepted as fact. I am one witness, and my Father who sent me is the other."

"Where is your father?" they asked.

Jesus answered, "Since you don't know who I am, you don't know who my Father is. If you knew me, you would also know my Father." Jesus made these statements while he was teaching in the section of the Temple known as the Treasury. But he was not arrested, because his time had not yet come.

#WalkWithJesus.—There will be times when you won't know which way to turn. Jesus said, "I am the light of the world. If you follow me, you won't have to walk in darkness, because you will have the light that leads to life." Come follow Jesus. He will show you where to go.

The Hope Of Eternal Life Comes Through Jesus
- John 8:21-59

Later Jesus said to them again, "I am going away. You will search for me but will die in your sin. You cannot come where I am going."

The people asked, "Is he planning to commit suicide? What does he mean, 'You cannot come where I am going'?"

Jesus continued, "You are from below; I am from above. You belong to this world; I do not. That is why I said that you will die in your sins; for unless you believe that I Am who I claim to be, you will die in your sins."

"Who are you?" they demanded.

Jesus replied, "The one I have always claimed to be. I have much to say about you and much to condemn, but I won't. For I say only what I have heard from the one who sent me, and he is completely truthful." But they still didn't understand that he was talking about his Father.

So Jesus said, "When you have lifted up the Son of Man on the cross, then you will understand that I Am he. I do nothing on my own but say only what the Father taught me. And the one who sent me is with me—he has not deserted me. For I always do what pleases him." Then many who heard him say these things believed in him.

Jesus said to the people who believed in him, "You are truly my disciples if you remain faithful to my teachings. And you will know the truth, and the truth will set you free."

"But we are descendants of Abraham," they said. "We have never been slaves to anyone. What do you mean, 'You will be set free'?"

Jesus replied, "I tell you the truth, everyone who sins is a slave of sin. A slave is not a permanent member of the family, but a son is part of the family forever. So if the Son sets you free, you are truly free. Yes, I realize that you are descendants of Abraham. And yet some of you are trying to kill me because there's no room in your hearts for my message. I am telling you what I saw when I was with my Father. But you are following the advice of your father."

"Our father is Abraham!" they declared.

"No," Jesus replied, "for if you were really the children of Abraham, you would follow his example. Instead, you are trying to kill me because I told you the truth, which I heard from God. Abraham never did such a thing. No, you are imitating your real father."

They replied, "We aren't illegitimate children! God himself is our true Father."

Jesus told them, "If God were your Father, you would love me, because I have come to you from God. I am not here on my own, but he sent me. Why can't you understand what I am saying? It's because you can't even hear me! For you are the children of your father the devil, and you love to do the evil things he does. He was a murderer from the beginning. He has always hated the truth, because there is no truth in him. When he lies, it is consistent with his character; for he is a liar and the father of lies. So when I tell the truth, you just naturally don't believe me! Which of you can truthfully accuse me of sin? And since I am telling you the truth, why don't you believe me? Anyone who belongs to God listens gladly to the words of God. But you don't listen because you don't belong to God."

The people retorted, "You Samaritan devil! Didn't we say all along that you were possessed by a demon?"

"No," Jesus said, "I have no demon in me. For I honor my Father—and you dishonor me. And though I have no wish to glorify myself, God is going to glorify me. He is the true judge. I tell you the truth, anyone who obeys my teaching will never die!"

The people said, "Now we know you are possessed by a demon. Even Abraham and the prophets died, but you say, 'Anyone who obeys my teaching will never die!' Are you greater than our father Abraham? He died, and so did the prophets. Who do you think you are?"

Jesus answered, "If I want glory for myself, it doesn't count. But it is my Father who will glorify me. You say, 'He is our God,' but you don't even know him. I know him. If I said otherwise, I would be as great a liar as you! But I do know him and obey him. Your father Abraham rejoiced as he looked forward to my coming. He saw it and was glad."

The people said, "You aren't even fifty years old. How can you say you have seen Abraham?"

Jesus answered, "I tell you the truth, before Abraham was even born, I Am!" At that point they picked up stones to throw at him. But Jesus was hidden from them and left the Temple.

#TrustJesus.—Know this, when you complain about circumstances because you don't see Jesus' larger plan for your life, yield your circumstances to Him. Open your eyes to see His plan for your life. Will you let Him take your problems and turn them into solutions?

9

The Power of Healing Leads to Hope

Jesus Gave Hope to the Blind Man - John 9:1-34

As Jesus was walking along, he saw a man who had been blind from birth. "Rabbi," his disciples asked him, "why was this man born blind? Was it because of his own sins or his parents' sins?"

"It was not because of his sins or his parents' sins," Jesus answered. "This happened so the power of God could be seen in him. We must quickly carry out the tasks assigned us by the one who sent us. The night is coming, and then no one can work. But while I am here in the world, I am the light of the world."

Then he spit on the ground, made mud with the saliva, and spread the mud over the blind man's eyes. He told him, "Go wash yourself in the pool of Siloam" (Siloam means "sent"). So the man went and washed and came back seeing!

His neighbors and others who knew him as a blind beggar asked each other, "Isn't this the man who used to sit and beg?" Some said he was, and others said, "No, he just looks like him!"

But the beggar kept saying, "Yes, I am the same one!"

They asked, "Who healed you? What happened?"

He told them, "The man they call Jesus made mud and spread it over my eyes and told me, 'Go to the pool of Siloam and wash yourself.' So I went and washed, and now I can see!"

"Where is he now?" they asked.

"I don't know," he replied.

Then they took the man who had been blind to the Pharisees, because it was on the Sabbath that Jesus had made the mud and healed him. The Pharisees asked the man all about it. So he told them, "He put the mud over my eyes, and when I washed it away, I could see!"

Some of the Pharisees said, "This man Jesus is not from God, for he is working on the Sabbath." Others said, "But how could an ordinary sinner do such miraculous signs?" So there was a deep division of opinion among them.

Then the Pharisees again questioned the man who had been blind and demanded, "What's your opinion about this man who healed you?"

The man replied, "I think he must be a prophet."

The Jewish leaders still refused to believe the man had been blind and could now see, so they called in his parents. They asked them, "Is this your son? Was he born blind? If so, how can he now see?"

His parents replied, "We know this is our son and that he was born blind, but we don't know how he can see or who healed him. Ask him. He is old enough to speak for himself." His parents said this because they were afraid of the Jewish leaders, who had announced that anyone saying Jesus was the Messiah would be expelled from the synagogue. That's why they said, "He is old enough. Ask him."

So for the second time they called in the man who had been blind and told him, "God should get the glory for this, because we know this man Jesus is a sinner."

"I don't know whether he is a sinner," the man replied. "But I know this: I was blind, and now I can see!"

"But what did he do?" they asked. "How did he heal you?"

"Look!" the man exclaimed. "I told you once. Didn't you listen? Why do you want to hear it again? Do you want to become his disciples, too?"

Then they cursed him and said, "You are his disciple, but we are disciples of Moses! We know God spoke to Moses, but we don't even know where this man comes from."

"Why, that's very strange!" the man replied. "He healed my eyes, and yet you don't know where he comes from? We know that God doesn't listen to sinners, but he is ready to hear those who worship him and do his will. Ever since the world began, no one has been able to open the eyes of someone born blind. If this man were not from God, he couldn't have done it."

"You were born a total sinner!" they answered. "Are you trying to teach us?" And they threw him out of the synagogue.

#TrustJesus.—While others moved away, Jesus saw a man that was blind from birth and moved toward him. Jesus is all about opening our eyes to see that suffering can only have real meaning in relation to God. God must be valued more than health and life itself. Like Jesus, see people with human challenges and move toward them.

Jesus Does Not Condemn but Gives Hope - John 9:35-41

When Jesus heard what had happened, he found the man and asked, "Do you believe in the Son of Man?"

The man answered, "Who is he, sir? I want to believe in him."

"You have seen him," Jesus said, "and he is speaking to you!"

"Yes, Lord, I believe!" the man said. And he worshiped Jesus.

Then Jesus told him, "I entered this world to render judgment—to give sight to the blind and to show those who think they see that they are blind."

Some Pharisees who were standing nearby heard him and asked, "Are you saying we're blind?"

"If you were blind, you wouldn't be guilty," Jesus replied. "But you remain guilty because you claim you can see.

#WalkWithJesus.—This Sixth Sign miracle proves Jesus is light, both physical and spiritual, having power over the physical body. Know this, Jesus' healing power demonstrates that He is all powerful. His care and concern shows that He is all loving. Will you show His kindness to everyone you come in contact with, and pray for His healing power in your life?

#YourTurn.—Jesus, starting today, I will focus on becoming a more caring person to the people I meet, using your example.

71

10

Jesus is the Door to Hope

Every hope we have is in the person of the Lord Jesus Christ. He is the only entrance to heaven. He is our shepherd Who looks after us. And He has a personal relationship with each person who comes to Him for salvation.

Do You Hear His Voice? - John 10:1-21

"I tell you the truth, anyone who sneaks over the wall of a sheepfold, rather than going through the gate, must surely be a thief and a robber! But the one who enters through the gate is the shepherd of the sheep. The gatekeeper opens the gate for him, and the sheep recognize his voice and come to him. He calls his own sheep by name and leads them out. After he has gathered his own flock, he walks ahead of them, and they follow him because they know his voice. They won't follow a stranger; they will run from him because they don't know his voice."

Those who heard Jesus use this illustration didn't understand what he meant, so he explained it to them: "I tell you the truth, I am the gate for the sheep. All who came before me were thieves and robbers. But the true sheep did not listen to them. Yes, I am the gate. Those who come in through me will be saved. They will come and go freely and will find good pastures. The thief's purpose is to steal and kill and destroy. My purpose is to give them a rich and satisfying life.

"I am the good shepherd. The good shepherd sacrifices his life for the sheep. A hired hand will run when he sees a wolf coming. He will abandon the sheep because they don't belong to him and he isn't their shepherd. And so the wolf attacks them and scatters the flock. The hired hand runs away because he's working only for the money and doesn't really care about the sheep.

"I am the good shepherd; I know my own sheep, and they know me, just as my Father knows me and I know the Father. So I sacrifice my life for the sheep. I have other sheep, too, that are not in this sheepfold. I must bring them also. They will listen to my voice, and there will be one flock with one shepherd.

"The Father loves me because I sacrifice my life so I may take it back again. No one can take my life from me. I sacrifice it voluntarily. For I have the authority to lay it down when I want to and also to take it up again. For this is what my Father has commanded."

When he said these things, the people were again divided in their opinions about him. Some said, "He's demon possessed and out of his mind. Why listen to a man like that?" Others said, "This doesn't sound like a man possessed by a demon! Can a demon open the eyes of the blind?"

#WalkWithJesus.—Jesus promises that if you enter the Door of salvation, you will enjoy the freedom of coming and going into His sheepfold. Also, He promises that you will enjoy life more abundantly. If you pray for salvation, you will enjoy fellowship with Jesus for eternity in a place called Heaven. Will you trust Jesus today?

The Father and I are One - John 10:22-30

It was now winter, and Jesus was in Jerusalem at the time of Hanukkah, the Festival of Dedication. He was in the Temple, walking through the section known as Solomon's Colonnade. The people surrounded him and asked, "How long are you going to keep us in suspense? If you are the Messiah, tell us plainly."

Jesus replied, "I have already told you, and you don't believe me. The proof is the work I do in my Father's name. But you don't believe me because you are not my sheep. My sheep listen to my voice; I know them, and they follow me. I give them eternal life, and they will never perish. No one can snatch them away from me, for my Father has given them to me, and he is more powerful than anyone else. No one can snatch them from the Father's hand. The Father and I are one."

#TrustJesus.—One of the greatest comforts in life is this; Jesus knows you by name, personally for all eternity. In fact, the Bible says that if you have trusted Jesus as your Savior, your name is written down in *"The Book of Life* in Heaven."* Is your name written down in glory? Have you believed in Him? Why not trust Him right now as He speaks to you?

Jesus is Rejected Because He And the Father Are One
- John 10:31-42

Once again the people picked up stones to kill him. Jesus said, "At my Father's direction I have done many good works. For which one are you going to stone me?"

They replied, "We're stoning you not for any good work, but for blasphemy! You, a mere man, claim to be God."

Jesus replied, "It is written in your own Scriptures that God said to certain leaders of the people, 'I say, you are gods!' And you know that the Scriptures cannot be altered. So if those people who received God's message were called 'gods,' why do you call it blasphemy when I say, 'I am the Son of God'? After all, the Father set me apart and sent me into the world. Don't believe me unless I carry out my Father's work. But if I do his work, believe in the evidence of the miraculous works I have done, even if you don't believe me. Then you will know and understand that the Father is in me, and I am in the Father."

Once again they tried to arrest him, but he got away and left them. He went beyond the Jordan River near the place where John was first baptizing and stayed there awhile. And many followed him. "John didn't perform miraculous signs," they remarked to one another, "but everything he said about this man has come true." And many who were there believed in Jesus.

#TrustJesus.—"God saved you by His grace through faith. And you can't take credit for this; it is a gift from God. Salvation is not a reward for the good things we have done, so none of us can boast about it." You must first place your complete trust in Jesus, not only for this life but for the life to come. Will you accept God's free gift of faith and believe in Jesus today for eternal life?

#YourTurn.—Jesus, I want to accept You as my Savior, and enjoy fellowshipping with You for eternity in heaven. Forgive me of my sins and come into my heart right now. I place my complete trust in You, and I accept Your free gift of eternal life today.

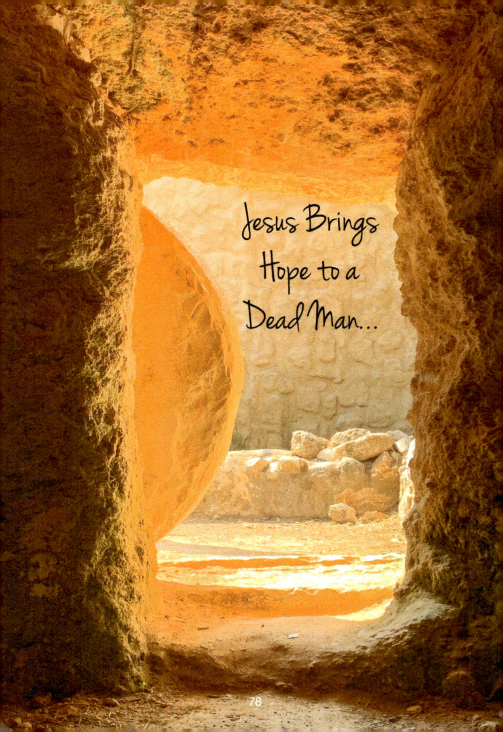

Jesus Brings
Hope to a
Dead Man...

Jesus Can Raise You to New Life

Only God Can Raise the Dead - John 11:1-16

A man named Lazarus was sick. He lived in Bethany with his sisters, Mary and Martha. This is the Mary who later poured the expensive perfume on the Lord's feet and wiped them with her hair. Her brother, Lazarus, was sick. So the two sisters sent a message to Jesus telling him, "Lord, your dear friend is very sick."

But when Jesus heard about it he said, "Lazarus's sickness will not end in death. No, it happened for the glory of God so that the Son of God will receive glory from this." So although Jesus loved Martha, Mary, and Lazarus, he stayed where he was for the next two days. Finally, he said to his disciples, "Let's go back to Judea."

But his disciples objected. "Rabbi," they said, "only a few days ago the people in Judea were trying to stone you. Are you going there again?"

Jesus replied, "There are twelve hours of daylight every day. During the day people can walk safely. They can see because they have the light of this world. But at night there is danger of stumbling because they have no light." Then he said, "Our friend Lazarus has fallen asleep, but now I will go and wake him up."

The disciples said, "Lord, if he is sleeping, he will soon get better!" They thought Jesus meant Lazarus was simply sleeping, but Jesus meant Lazarus had died.

So he told them plainly, "Lazarus is dead. And for your sakes, I'm glad I wasn't there, for now you will really believe. Come, let's go see him."

Thomas, nicknamed the Twin, said to his fellow disciples, "Let's go, too—and die with Jesus."

#TrustJesus.—None of us are strangers to death. As we live our life, we will have family and friends die around us. By placing your trust in Jesus, you can be prepared for eternal life with Him.

I Am the Resurrection and the Life - John 11:17-27

When Jesus arrived at Bethany, he was told that Lazarus had already been in his grave for four days. Bethany was only a few miles down the road from Jerusalem, and many of the people had come to console Martha and Mary in their loss. When Martha got word that Jesus was coming, she went to meet him. But Mary stayed in the house. Martha said to Jesus, "Lord, if only you had been here, my brother would not have died. But even now I know that God will give you whatever you ask."

Jesus told her, "Your brother will rise again."

"Yes," Martha said, "he will rise when everyone else rises, at the last day."

Jesus told her, "I am the resurrection and the life. Anyone who believes in me will live, even after dying. Everyone who lives in me and believes in me will never ever die. Do you believe this, Martha?"

"Yes, Lord," she told him. "I have always believed you are the Messiah, the Son of God, the one who has come into the world from God."

#TrustJesus.—Jesus said that He possessed the divine power to bring the dead to life. The one who believes in Jesus has eternal life that transcends physical death. Jesus tells us that at death the Christian makes an instant transition from the old, earthly life to the new, eternal, heavenly life.

Lazarus Come Out! - John 11:28-44

Then she returned to Mary. She called Mary aside from the mourners and told her, "The Teacher is here and wants to see you." So Mary immediately went to him.

Jesus had stayed outside the village, at the place where Martha met him. When the people who were at the house consoling Mary saw her leave so hastily, they assumed she was going to Lazarus's grave to weep. So they followed her there. When Mary arrived and saw Jesus, she fell at his feet and said, "Lord, if only you had been here, my brother would not have died."

When Jesus saw her weeping and saw the other people wailing with her, a deep anger welled up within him, and he was deeply troubled. "Where have you put him?" he asked them.

They told him, "Lord, come and see." Then Jesus wept. The people who were standing nearby said, "See how much he loved him!" But some said, "This man healed a blind man. Couldn't he have kept Lazarus from dying?"

Jesus was still angry as he arrived at the tomb, a cave with a stone rolled across its entrance. "Roll the stone aside," Jesus told them.

But Martha, the dead man's sister, protested, "Lord, he has been dead for four days. The smell will be terrible."

Jesus responded, "Didn't I tell you that you would see God's glory if you believe?" So they rolled the stone aside. Then Jesus looked up to heaven and said, "Father, thank you for hearing me. You always hear me, but I said it out loud for the sake of all these people standing here, so that they will believe you sent me." Then Jesus shouted, "Lazarus, come out!" And the dead man came out, his hands and feet bound in graveclothes, his face wrapped in a headcloth. Jesus told them, "Unwrap him and let him go!"

#TrustJesus.—This seventh sign miracle proves that Jesus overcomes death, having power over life and eternity. Only God can raise the dead to life. Jesus raised Lazarus to life after he had been dead four days. He will do the same for you, so that you can live with Him in Heaven forever. Will you place your trust in Jesus today?

The Plot to Kill Jesus - John 11:45-57

Many of the people who were with Mary believed in Jesus when they saw this happen. But some went to the Pharisees and told them what Jesus had done. Then the leading priests and Pharisees called the high council together. "What are we going to do?" they asked each other. "This man certainly performs many miraculous signs. If we allow him to go on like this, soon everyone will believe in him. Then the Roman army will come and destroy both our Temple and our nation."

Caiaphas, who was high priest at that time, said, "You don't know what you're talking about! You don't realize that it's better for you that one man should die for the people than for the whole nation to be destroyed."

He did not say this on his own; as high priest at that time he was led to prophesy that Jesus would die for the entire nation. And not only for that nation, but to bring together and unite all the children of God scattered around the world.

So from that time on, the Jewish leaders began to plot Jesus' death. As a result, Jesus stopped his public ministry among the people and left Jerusalem. He went to a place near the wilderness, to the village of Ephraim, and stayed there with his disciples.

It was now almost time for the Jewish Passover celebration, and many people from all over the country arrived in Jerusalem several days early so they could go through the purification ceremony before Passover began. They kept looking for Jesus, but as they stood around in the Temple, they said to each other, "What do you think? He won't come for Passover, will he?" Meanwhile, the leading priests and Pharisees had publicly ordered that anyone seeing Jesus must report it immediately so they could arrest him.

#TrustJesus.—Allow Jesus to sit on the throne of your heart to rule all you say and do. He wants to give you an abundant life; not only in this life, but the life to come.

12

Many Believe the Message of Hope

Mary Anointed Jesus' Feet at a Banquet in Bethany - John 12:1-11

Six days before the Passover celebration began, Jesus arrived in Bethany, the home of Lazarus—the man he had raised from the dead. A dinner was prepared in Jesus' honor. Martha served, and Lazarus was among those who ate with him. Then Mary took a twelve-ounce jar of expensive perfume made from essence of nard, and she anointed Jesus' feet with it, wiping his feet with her hair. The house was filled with the fragrance.

But Judas Iscariot, the disciple who would soon betray him, said, "That perfume was worth a year's wages. It should have been sold and the money given to the poor." Not that he cared for the poor—he was a thief, and since he was in charge of the disciples' money, he often stole some for himself.

Jesus replied, "Leave her alone. She did this in preparation for my burial. You will always have the poor among you, but you will not always have me."

When all the people heard of Jesus' arrival, they flocked to see him and also to see Lazarus, the man Jesus had raised from the dead. Then the leading priests decided to kill Lazarus, too, for it was because of him that many of the people had deserted them and believed in Jesus.

#TrustJesus.—Jesus knows your thoughts, just as He knew the religious leaders' thoughts when He was on this earth. He will forgive you for any sin or doubt that hides in your heart. Will you let Him teach you to think His thoughts?

Jesus Entered Jerusalem as Messiah - John 12:12-19

The next day, the news that Jesus was on the way to Jerusalem swept through the city. A large crowd of Passover visitors took palm branches and went down the road to meet him. They shouted,

"Praise God!
Blessings on the one who comes in the name of the LORD!
Hail to the King of Israel!"

Jesus found a young donkey and rode on it, fulfilling the prophecy that said:

"Don't be afraid, people of Jerusalem.
Look, your King is coming, riding on a donkey's colt."

His disciples didn't understand at the time that this was a fulfillment of prophecy. But after Jesus entered into his glory, they remembered what had happened and realized that these things had been written about him.

Many in the crowd had seen Jesus call Lazarus from the tomb, raising him from the dead, and they were telling others about it. That was the reason so many went out to meet him—because they had heard about this miraculous sign. Then the Pharisees said to each other, "There's nothing we can do. Look, everyone has gone after him!"

#TrustJesus.—Will you follow Jesus wherever He leads? He will give you a willing spirit, courage to endure, and strength to do it.

The Father Spoke to Jesus From Heaven - John 12:20-41

Some Greeks who had come to Jerusalem for the Passover celebration paid a visit to Philip, who was from Bethsaida in Galilee. They said, "Sir, we want to meet Jesus." Philip told Andrew about it, and they went together to ask Jesus.

Jesus replied, "Now the time has come for the Son of Man to enter into his glory. I tell you the truth, unless a kernel of wheat is planted in the soil and dies, it remains alone. But its death will produce many new kernels—a plentiful harvest of new lives. Those who love their life in this world will lose it. Those who care nothing for their life in this world will keep it for eternity. Anyone who wants to serve me must follow me, because my servants must be where I am. And the Father will honor anyone who serves me.

"Now my soul is deeply troubled. Should I pray, 'Father, save me from this hour'? But this is the very reason I came! Father, bring glory to your name."

Then a voice spoke from heaven, saying, "I have already brought glory to my name, and I will do so again." When the crowd heard the voice, some thought it was thunder, while others declared an angel had spoken to him.

Then Jesus told them, "The voice was for your benefit, not mine. The time for judging this world has come, when Satan, the ruler of this world, will be cast out. And when I am lifted up from the earth, I will draw everyone to myself." He said this to indicate how he was going to die.

The crowd responded, "We understood from Scripture that the Messiah would live forever. How can you say the Son of Man will die? Just who is this Son of Man, anyway?"

Jesus replied, "My light will shine for you just a little longer. Walk in the light while you can, so the darkness will not overtake you. Those who walk in the darkness cannot see where they are going. Put your trust in the light while there is still time; then you will become children of the light."

After saying these things, Jesus went away and was hidden from them.

But despite all the miraculous signs Jesus had done, most of the people still did not believe in him. This is exactly what Isaiah the prophet had predicted:

"LORD, who has believed our message?
To whom has the LORD revealed his powerful arm?"

But the people couldn't believe, for as Isaiah also said,

"The Lord has blinded their eyes
and hardened their hearts—
so that their eyes cannot see,
and their hearts cannot understand,
and they cannot turn to me
and have me heal them."

Isaiah was referring to Jesus when he said this, because he saw the future and spoke of the Messiah's glory.

#TrustJesus.—"Let your light so shine before men, that they may see your good works and glorify your Father in heaven." Placing your trust in Jesus, allows Him to show His light to a world in darkness and without hope. When people see you they will see Jesus.

Walk in the Light of Hope - John 12:42-50

Many people did believe in him, however, including some of the Jewish leaders. But they wouldn't admit it for fear that the Pharisees would expel them from the synagogue. For they loved human praise more than the praise of God.

Jesus shouted to the crowds, "If you trust me, you are trusting not only me, but also God who sent me. For when you see me, you are seeing the one who sent me. I have come as a light to shine in this dark world, so that all who put their trust in me will no longer remain in the dark. I will not judge those who hear me but don't obey me, for I have come to save the world and not to judge it. But all who reject me and my message will be judged on the day of judgment by the truth I have spoken. I don't speak on my own authority. The Father who sent me has commanded me what to say and how to say it. And I know his commands lead to eternal life; so I say whatever the Father tells me to say."

> #TrustJesus.—You are saved by grace because you put your faith in Jesus. It is not your own doing, but His gift to you. You cannot boast that you had anything to do with it. He will make you a new person created in Him to serve God. You don't deserve salvation, because of your past sins, but God will give you the greatest gift of all—salvation. Then He will equip you to serve with good works. Will you accept His free gift of eternal life today?

13

The Humility of Jesus Shows Hope

Throughout his life on earth, Jesus demonstrated a spirit of profound humility, saying that He "came not to be served but to serve others and to give his life as a ransom for many." "So humble yourselves under the mighty power of God, and at the right time he will lift you up in honor." This gives us hope and encouragement.

Jesus Washed His Disciples Feet - John 13:1-20

Before the Passover celebration, Jesus knew that his hour had come to leave this world and return to his Father. He had loved his disciples during his ministry on earth, and now he loved them to the very end. It was time for supper, and the devil had already prompted Judas, son of Simon Iscariot, to betray Jesus. Jesus knew that the Father had given him authority over everything and that he had come from God and would return to God. So he got up from the table, took off his robe, wrapped a towel around his waist, and poured water into a basin. Then he began to wash the disciples' feet, drying them with the towel he had around him.

When Jesus came to Simon Peter, Peter said to him, "Lord, are you going to wash my feet?"

Jesus replied, "You don't understand now what I am doing, but someday you will."

"No," Peter protested, "you will never ever wash my feet!"

Jesus replied, "Unless I wash you, you won't belong to me."

Simon Peter exclaimed, "Then wash my hands and head as well, Lord, not just my feet!"

Jesus replied, "A person who has bathed all over does not need to wash, except for the feet, to be entirely clean. And you disciples are clean, but not all of you." For Jesus knew who would betray him. That is what he meant when he said, "Not all of you are clean."

After washing their feet, he put on his robe again and sat down and asked, "Do you understand what I was doing? You call me 'Teacher' and 'Lord,' and you are right, because that's what I am. And since I, your Lord and Teacher, have washed your feet, you ought to wash each other's feet. I have given you an example to follow. Do as I have done to you. I tell you the truth, slaves are not greater than their master. Nor is the messenger more important than the one who sends the message. Now that you know these things, God will bless you for doing them.

"I am not saying these things to all of you; I know the ones I have chosen. But this fulfills the Scripture that says, 'The one who eats my food has turned against me.' I tell you this beforehand, so that when it happens you will believe that I Am the Messiah. I tell you the truth, anyone who welcomes my messenger is welcoming me, and anyone who welcomes me is welcoming the Father who sent me."

#WalkWithJesus.—Just as Jesus washed the feet of His followers, He will help you to be humble and serve others. Will you follow His example and serve others?

Judas Betrayed Jesus, But You Can Believe
- John 13:21-30

Now Jesus was deeply troubled, and he exclaimed, "I tell you the truth, one of you will betray me!"

The disciples looked at each other, wondering whom he could mean. The disciple Jesus loved was sitting next to Jesus at the table. Simon Peter motioned to him to ask, "Who's he talking about?"

So that disciple leaned over to Jesus and asked, "Lord, who is it?"

Jesus responded, "It is the one to whom I give the bread I dip in the bowl." And when he had dipped it, he gave it to Judas, son of Simon Iscariot. When Judas had eaten the bread, Satan entered into him. Then Jesus told him, "Hurry and do what you're going to do." None of the others at the table knew what Jesus meant. Since Judas was their treasurer, some thought Jesus was telling him to go and pay for the food or to give some money to the poor.

So Judas left at once, going out into the night.

#WalkWithJesus.—One of Jesus' disciples chose to betray Him. You can choose a path to life. The call to follow Jesus is a call to follow Him and trust the course that He sets even when it seems that it's not "working." Stop and think about this: Jesus loved you enough to die for you. And he loves you just as much, no matter how many times you stumble and fall and weep and turn back. He takes your guilt and makes it so that in God's sight you never sinned. That's the kind of friend you need, but can never deserve. Yet in Jesus, that is the kind of friend we have.

Jesus Gave a New Commandment - John 13:31-38

As soon as Judas left the room, Jesus said, "The time has come for the Son of Man to enter into his glory, and God will be glorified because of him. And since God receives glory because of the Son, he will give his own glory to the Son, and he will do so at once. Dear children, I will be with you only a little longer. And as I told the Jewish leaders, you will search for me, but you can't come where I am going. So now I am giving you a new commandment: Love each other. Just as I have loved you, you should love each other. Your love for one another will prove to the world that you are my disciples."

Simon Peter asked, "Lord, where are you going?"

And Jesus replied, "You can't go with me now, but you will follow me later."

"But why can't I come now, Lord?" he asked. "I'm ready to die for you."

Jesus answered, "Die for me? I tell you the truth, Peter—before the rooster crows tomorrow morning, you will deny three times that you even know me.

#LoveJesus.—Everyone, in their lifetime, has difficulty loving some people. Jesus loves everyone in the whole world and died for them. When you encounter those who are difficult to love, let Jesus love them through you. Will you allow Him to demonstrate to the world true Christian love, so they will know you are His follower because of your love?

14

The Promise of Jesus
Seals the Hope in Us

Along with the gift of salvation, Jesus also gives us promises. These promises center around what is promised to us in heaven, how the Father also loves us, and the ministry of comfort the Holy Spirit gives us. And the good thing is that it is all free to us!

You Can be Comforted With the Truth - John 14:1-7

llDon't let your hearts be troubled. Trust in God, and trust also in me. There is more than enough room in my Father's home. If this were not so, would I have told you that I am going to prepare a place for you? When everything is ready, I will come and get you, so that you will always be with me where I am. And you know the way to where I am going."

"No, we don't know, Lord," Thomas said. "We have no idea where you are going, so how can we know the way?"

Jesus told him, "I am the way, the truth, and the life. No one can come to the Father except through me. If you had really known me, you would know who my Father is. From now on, you do know him and have seen him!"

#TrustJesus.—Jesus said that He would come back to take you where He is. That's what He wants. He wants you to live with Him in heaven for all eternity. Will you accept His gift today?

To Know Jesus is to Know His Father - John 14:8-14

Philip said, "Lord, show us the Father, and we will be satisfied."

Jesus replied, "Have I been with you all this time, Philip, and yet you still don't know who I am? Anyone who has seen me has seen the Father! So why are you asking me to show him to you? Don't you believe that I am in the Father and the Father is in me? The words I speak are not my own, but my Father who lives in me does his work through me. Just believe that I am in the Father and the Father is in me. Or at least believe because of the work you have seen me do.

"I tell you the truth, anyone who believes in me will do the same works I have done, and even greater works, because I am going to be with the Father. You can ask for anything in my name, and I will do it, so that the Son can bring glory to the Father. Yes, ask me for anything in my name, and I will do it!

#TrustJesus.—Will you come in the name of Jesus, to ask your request? He said that He would do it if you asked in His name. If you have placed your complete trust in Jesus, you can ask in His name because He is in your heart. His blood has cleansed you and has given you access to His Father because He is your intercessor. Trust in Him today.

Your Promise for Today and Tomorrow - John 14:15-21

❝❞If you love me, obey my commandments. And I will ask the Father, and he will give you another Advocate, who will never leave you. He is the Holy Spirit, who leads into all truth. The world cannot receive him, because it isn't looking for him and doesn't recognize him. But you know him, because he lives with you now and later will be in you. No, I will not abandon you as orphans—I will come to you. Soon the world will no longer see me, but you will see me. Since I live, you also will live. When I am raised to life again, you will know that I am in my Father, and you are in me, and I am in you. Those who accept my commandments and obey them are the ones who love me. And because they love me, my Father will love them. And I will love them and reveal myself to each of them."

#TrustJesus.—Jesus promised two things that you can know beyond a shadow of a doubt: first, He would come to live within your heart when you are saved; second, you would be placed in Him in heaven. The first means you have His life in you. The second means you can be as close to God, the heavenly Father, as Jesus is. Will you come to Jesus today?

I Am Leaving you With a Gift
- John 14:22-31

Judas (not Judas Iscariot, but the other disciple with that name) said to him, "Lord, why are you going to reveal yourself only to us and not to the world at large?"

Jesus replied, "All who love me will do what I say. My Father will love them, and we will come and make our home with each of them. Anyone who doesn't love me will not obey me. And remember, my words are not my own. What I am telling you is from the Father who sent me. I am telling you these things now while I am still with you. But when the Father sends the Advocate as my representative—that is, the Holy Spirit—he will teach you everything and will remind you of everything I have told you.

"I am leaving you with a gift—peace of mind and heart. And the peace I give is a gift the world cannot give. So don't be troubled or afraid. Remember what I told you: I am going away, but I will come back to you again. If you really loved me, you would be happy that I am going to the Father, who is greater than I am. I have told you these things before they happen so that when they do happen, you will believe.

"I don't have much more time to talk to you, because the ruler of this world approaches. He has no power over me, but I will do what the Father requires of me, so that the world will know that I love the Father. Come, let's be going.

#WalkWithJesus.—You need the Holy Spirit guiding in your life to help you learn Scripture and to remember the things Jesus said.

15

The Hope Living in You Brings Joy

Remain in My Love - John 15:1-13

*"*I am the true grapevine, and my Father is the gardener. He cuts off every branch of mine that doesn't produce fruit, and he prunes the branches that do bear fruit so they will produce even more. You have already been pruned and purified by the message I have given you. Remain in me, and I will remain in you. For a branch cannot produce fruit if it is severed from the vine, and you cannot be fruitful unless you remain in me.

"Yes, I am the vine; you are the branches. Those who remain in me, and I in them, will produce much fruit. For apart from me you can do nothing. Anyone who does not remain in me is thrown away like a useless branch and withers. Such branches are gathered into a pile to be burned. But if you remain in me and my words remain in you, you may ask for anything you want, and it will be granted! When you produce much fruit, you are my true disciples. This brings great glory to my Father.

"I have loved you even as the Father has loved me. Remain in my love. When you obey my commandments, you remain in my love, just as I obey my Father's commandments and remain in his love. I have told you these things so that you will be filled with my joy. Yes, your joy will overflow! This is my commandment: Love each other in the same way I have loved you. There is no greater love than to lay down one's life for one's friends.

#WalkWithJesus.—Jesus wants you to produce more fruit in your Christian life, and more fruit in your service to Him. He wants you to abide in Him so you can be fruitful.

#YourTurn.—Jesus, help me to surrender my will to Your will. I want to live according to Your Word so that I can love my friends and family with Your love.

You are My Friends - John 15:14-27

You are my friends if you do what I command. I no longer call you slaves, because a master doesn't confide in his slaves. Now you are my friends, since I have told you everything the Father told me. You didn't choose me. I chose you. I appointed you to go and produce lasting fruit, so that the Father will give you whatever you ask for, using my name. This is my command: Love each other.

"If the world hates you, remember that it hated me first. The world would love you as one of its own if you belonged to it, but you are no longer part of the world. I chose you to come out of the world, so it hates you. Do you remember what I told you? 'A slave is not greater than the master.' Since they persecuted me, naturally they will persecute you. And if they had listened to me, they would listen to you. They will do all this to you because of me, for they have rejected the one who sent me. They would not be guilty if I had not come and spoken to them. But now they have no excuse for their sin. Anyone who hates me also hates my Father. If I hadn't done such miraculous signs among them that no one else could do, they would not be guilty. But as it is, they have seen everything I did, yet they still hate me and my Father. This fulfills what is written in their Scriptures: 'They hated me without cause.'

"But I will send you the Advocate—the Spirit of truth. He will come to you from the Father and will testify all about me. And you must also testify about me because you have been with me from the beginning of my ministry.

#TrustJesus.—Will you tell your friends and family about Jesus? He will speak through you and remove their blindness.

98

16

The Presence of Jesus in You is Your Hope

I Will Never Abandon You - John 16:1-7

❝I have told you these things so that you won't abandon your faith. For you will be expelled from the synagogues, and the time is coming when those who kill you will think they are doing a holy service for God. This is because they have never known the Father or me. Yes, I'm telling you these things now, so that when they happen, you will remember my warning. I didn't tell you earlier because I was going to be with you for a while longer.

"But now I am going away to the one who sent me, and not one of you is asking where I am going. Instead, you grieve because of what I've told you. But in fact, it is best for you that I go away, because if I don't, the Advocate won't come. If I do go away, then I will send him to you.

#LoveJesus.—The world will hate you, just as it hated Jesus. He will give you strength to endure persecution and live for Him. He will help you to do more than endure trials. He will give you victory over them, through the power of the Holy Spirit in you. Will you trust the power of the Holy Spirit in you?

The Holy Spirit Will Glorify Me - John 16:8-15

And when he comes, he will convict the world of its sin, and of God's righteousness, and of the coming judgment. The world's sin is that it refuses to believe in me. Righteousness is available because I go to the Father, and you will see me no more. Judgment will come because the ruler of this world has already been judged.

"There is so much more I want to tell you, but you can't bear it now. When the Spirit of truth comes, he will guide you into all truth. He will not speak on his own but will tell you what he has heard. He will tell you about the future. He will bring me glory by telling you whatever he receives from me. All that belongs to the Father is mine; this is why I said, 'The Spirit will tell you whatever he receives from me.'"

#WalkWithJesus.—Jesus will send the Holy Spirit to guide you into truth, and to keep you from error. The world, the flesh, and the devil continually try to pull you away from Him. But be not afraid, Jesus has overcome the world, the flesh, and the devil.

Ask and You Will Receive - John 16:16-24

"In a little while you won't see me anymore. But a little while after that, you will see me again."

Some of the disciples asked each other, "What does he mean when he says, 'In a little while you won't see me, but then you will see me,' and 'I am going to the Father'? And what does he mean by 'a little while'? We don't understand."

Jesus realized they wanted to ask him about it, so he said, "Are you asking yourselves what I meant? I said in a little while you won't see me, but a little while after that you will see me again. I tell you the truth, you will weep and mourn over what is going to happen to me, but the world will rejoice. You will grieve, but your grief will suddenly turn to wonderful joy. It will be like a woman suffering the pains of labor. When her child is born, her anguish gives way to joy because she has brought a new baby into the world. So you have sorrow now, but I will see you again; then you will rejoice, and no one can rob you of that joy. At that time you won't need to ask me for anything. I tell you the truth, you will ask the Father directly, and he will grant your request because you use my name. You haven't done this before. Ask, using my name, and you will receive, and you will have abundant joy.

> #WalkWithJesus.—When we truly desire God, when we are passionate to see His will accomplished in this world, and when we ask for what brings Him glory, He is eager to give us what we ask for. Sometimes the things that glorify God are pleasant. Sometimes they are difficult for us. But, when we pray within His will, in the authority of Jesus' name, persistently, unselfishly, and in faith, we will receive what we need.

I Have Overcome the World - John 16:25-33

"I have spoken of these matters in figures of speech, but soon I will stop speaking figuratively and will tell you plainly all about the Father. Then you will ask in my name. I'm not saying I will ask the Father on your behalf, for the Father himself loves you dearly because you love me and believe that I came from God. Yes, I came from the Father into the world, and now I will leave the world and return to the Father."

Then his disciples said, "At last you are speaking plainly and not figuratively. Now we understand that you know everything, and there's no need to question you. From this we believe that you came from God."

Jesus asked, "Do you finally believe? But the time is coming—indeed it's here now—when you will be scattered, each one going his own way, leaving me alone. Yet I am not alone because the Father is with me. I have told you all this so that you may have peace in me. Here on earth you will have many trials and sorrows. But take heart, because I have overcome the world."

#WalkWithJesus.—"You have heard it said to love your friends and hate your enemies. But I say do good to those who hate you and pray for those who despitefully use you. Treat them as you want to be treated, so that you will be of My heavenly Father, because He makes the sun rise on evil people and good people and sends rain on the evil and the good. If you love only those who love you, there is no spiritual reward in that. Even sinners love those who love them. Love your enemies and do good things to those who hate you, because I said, 'You would receive a rich reward, and should show everyone that you are a child of the Most High.'" Will you show love to those who hurt you?

17

The Prayer of Jesus For You Gives You Hope

Father, Glorify your Son - John 17:1-5

After saying all these things, Jesus looked up to heaven and said, "Father, the hour has come. Glorify your Son so he can give glory back to you. For you have given him authority over everyone. He gives eternal life to each one you have given him. And this is the way to have eternal life—to know you, the only true God, and Jesus Christ, the one you sent to earth. I brought glory to you here on earth by completing the work you gave me to do. Now, Father, bring me into the glory we shared before the world began.

> #WalkWithJesus.—Jesus came from heaven to the earth He created, and gave His life on the cross, and then He returned to His Father in heaven. He did all of this for you so that you could believe in Him and have eternal life. Will you believe that He is the Christ, and promise that you will love others as He loves you?

Make Them Holy by Your Truth - John 17:6-19

I have revealed you to the ones you gave me from this world. They were always yours. You gave them to me, and they have kept your word. Now they know that everything I have is a gift from you, for I have passed on to them the message you gave me. They accepted it and know that I came from you, and they believe you sent me.

"My prayer is not for the world, but for those you have given me, because they belong to you. All who are mine belong to you, and you have given them to me, so they bring me glory. Now I am departing from the world; they are staying in this world, but I am coming to you. Holy Father, you have given me your name; now protect them by the power of your name so that they will be united just as we are. During my time here, I protected them by the power of the name you gave me. I guarded them so that not one was lost, except the one headed for destruction, as the Scriptures foretold.

"Now I am coming to you. I told them many things while I was with them in this world so they would be filled with my joy. I have given them your word. And the world hates them because they do not belong to the world, just as I do not belong to the world. I'm not asking you to take them out of the world, but to keep them safe from the evil one. They do not belong to this world any more than I do. Make them holy by your truth; teach them your word, which is truth. Just as you sent me into the world, I am sending them into the world. And I give myself as a holy sacrifice for them so they can be made holy by your truth.

#WalkWithJesus.—Jesus wants you to know Him and to spend your life learning about Him, and telling your family and friends about what He did in your life. Then, one day, He will call you home to be with Him. So we ask you this question, "Whether in death or the rapture, will you accept Jesus today and live with Him for eternity in a place that He is preparing for you?

#YourTurn.—Jesus, I accept you as my Savior. Forgive me for my sins. I now receive your free gift of eternal life. I want all of my friends and family to know you like I do.

I Am Praying For All Who Will Ever Believe in Me
- John 17:20-26

❝I am praying not only for these disciples but also for all who will ever believe in me through their message. I pray that they will all be one, just as you and I are one—as you are in me, Father, and I am in you. And may they be in us so that the world will believe you sent me.

"I have given them the glory you gave me, so they may be one as we are one. I am in them and you are in me. May they experience such perfect unity that the world will know that you sent me and that you love them as much as you love me. Father, I want these whom you have given me to be with me where I am. Then they can see all the glory you gave me because you loved me even before the world began!

"O righteous Father, the world doesn't know you, but I do; and these disciples know you sent me. I have revealed you to them, and I will continue to do so. Then your love for me will be in them, and I will be in them."

#TrustJesus.—You can't begin to imagine the wonders and glory Jesus has waiting for you in heaven. There is a sparkling clean river, flowing from Jesus' and His Father's throne. A Tree of Life grows on each side of the river. There is nothing evil in the city because the Father's throne and Jesus' throne are there. Jesus' servants will worship Him continually. They will see His face and His name will be on their foreheads. And He will rule His people forever.

The Garden of Gethsemane

18

Jesus Died For You

The events in this chapter and the next chapter are the most important events in the history of the world. What He did here promises those who call upon Him that they will go to heaven for all eternity.

Who Are You Looking For? - John 18:1-12

After saying these things, Jesus crossed the Kidron Valley with his disciples and entered a grove of olive trees. Judas, the betrayer, knew this place, because Jesus had often gone there with his disciples. The leading priests and Pharisees had given Judas a contingent of Roman soldiers and Temple guards to accompany him. Now with blazing torches, lanterns, and weapons, they arrived at the olive grove.

Jesus fully realized all that was going to happen to him, so he stepped forward to meet them. "Who are you looking for?" he asked.

"Jesus the Nazarene," they replied.

"I Am he," Jesus said. (Judas, who betrayed him, was standing with them.) As Jesus said "I Am he," they all drew back and fell to the ground! Once more he asked them, "Who are you looking for?"

And again they replied, "Jesus the Nazarene."

"I told you that I Am he," Jesus said. "And since I am the one you want, let these others go." He did this to fulfill his own statement: "I did not lose a single one of those you have given me."

Then Simon Peter drew a sword and slashed off the right ear of Malchus, the high priest's slave. But Jesus said to Peter, "Put your sword back into its sheath. Shall I not drink from the cup of suffering the Father has given me?"

So the soldiers, their commanding officer, and the Temple guards arrested Jesus and tied him up.

#TrustJesus.—Jesus knows you are vulnerable if not protected by Him. But know this, He will never let you be tempted beyond what you can bear, but with every temptation He will make a way for you to escape. Is your security in your strength, or have you placed your trust in Jesus?

The First Trial Before The High Priest - John 18:13-23

First they took him to Annas, since he was the father-in-law of Caiaphas, the high priest at that time. Caiaphas was the one who had told the other Jewish leaders, "It's better that one man should die for the people."

Simon Peter followed Jesus, as did another of the disciples. That other disciple was acquainted with the high priest, so he was allowed to enter the high priest's courtyard with Jesus. Peter had to stay outside the gate. Then the disciple who knew the high priest spoke to the woman watching at the gate, and she let Peter in. The woman asked Peter, "You're not one of that man's disciples, are you?"

"No," he said, "I am not."

Because it was cold, the household servants and the guards had made a charcoal fire. They stood around it, warming themselves, and Peter stood with them, warming himself.

Inside, the high priest began asking Jesus about his followers and what he had been teaching them. Jesus replied, "Everyone knows what I teach. I have preached regularly in the synagogues and the Temple, where the people gather. I have not spoken in secret. Why are you asking me this question? Ask those who heard me. They know what I said."

Then one of the Temple guards standing nearby slapped Jesus across the face. "Is that the way to answer the high priest?" he demanded.

Jesus replied, "If I said anything wrong, you must prove it. But if I'm speaking the truth, why are you beating me?"

#TrustJesus.—When Jesus walked on this earth 2,000 years ago, He had no secret agenda; He had no secret doctrine; He was honest, open and transparent before a watching world. Those who heard Jesus preach, heard a clear message of hope. The message of good news to humankind was His life, death, and resurrection. Will you believe in the good news?

Peter Denied Jesus the Second and Third Time
- John 18:24-28

Then Annas bound Jesus and sent him to Caiaphas, the high priest. Meanwhile, as Simon Peter was standing by the fire warming himself, they asked him again, "You're not one of his disciples, are you?"

He denied it, saying, "No, I am not."

But one of the household slaves of the high priest, a relative of the man whose ear Peter had cut off, asked, "Didn't I see you out there in the olive grove with Jesus?" Again Peter denied it. And immediately a rooster crowed. Jesus' trial before Caiaphas ended in the early hours of the morning. Then he was taken to the headquarters of the Roman governor. His accusers didn't go inside because it would defile them, and they wouldn't be allowed to celebrate the Passover.

#TrustJesus.—Jesus knew Peter would deny Him. He also knew he would return to Him. It was His grace that brought Peter back. That same grace is available to you when you sin. This is your only hope of staying faith. You can have that assurance that Jesus will keep you from stumbling, and will lift you up to strengthen others. Will you trust Jesus today?

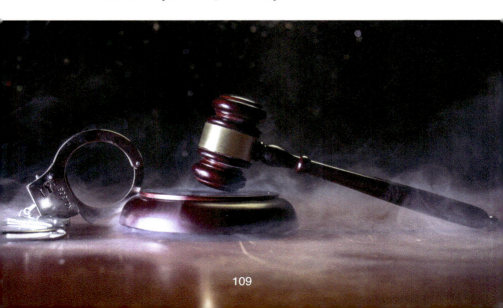

The Third Trial Before Pilate - John 18:29-40

So Pilate, the governor, went out to them and asked, "What is your charge against this man?"

"We wouldn't have handed him over to you if he weren't a criminal!" they retorted.

"Then take him away and judge him by your own law," Pilate told them.

"Only the Romans are permitted to execute someone," the Jewish leaders replied. (This fulfilled Jesus' prediction about the way he would die.)

Then Pilate went back into his headquarters and called for Jesus to be brought to him. "Are you the king of the Jews?" he asked him.

Jesus replied, "Is this your own question, or did others tell you about me?"

"Am I a Jew?" Pilate retorted. "Your own people and their leading priests brought you to me for trial. Why? What have you done?"

Jesus answered, "My Kingdom is not an earthly kingdom. If it were, my followers would fight to keep me from being handed over to the Jewish leaders. But my Kingdom is not of this world."

Pilate said, "So you are a king?"

Jesus responded, "You say I am a king. Actually, I was born and came into the world to testify to the truth. All who love the truth recognize that what I say is true."

"What is truth?" Pilate asked. Then he went out again to the people and told them, "He is not guilty of any crime. But you have a custom of asking me to release one prisoner each year at Passover. Would you like me to release this 'King of the Jews'?"

But they shouted back, "No! Not this man. We want Barabbas!" (Barabbas was a revolutionary.)

#TrustJesus.—Several hours before His death, Jesus makes a statement about His birth. The purpose of His birth was to bear witness to the truth of God, so that everyone might glorify God for who He is and might come to have eternal life. God is the author of all truth. To know the truth is to know Jesus, who is the very image and reflection of God. Is there a real longing in you for the truth? Jesus is saying, "If your will is humble enough to follow the truth, you will hear and know the words of truth."

19

The Preparation For Our Hope

The actions of the Lord Jesus Christ on the cross are the center and the pivot for all history. The death, burial and resurrection of the Lord Jesus Christ is the door for salvation for all who call upon His name.

I Find Him Not Guilty - John 19:1-7

Then Pilate had Jesus flogged with a lead-tipped whip. The soldiers wove a crown of thorns and put it on his head, and they put a purple robe on him. "Hail! King of the Jews!" they mocked, as they slapped him across the face.

Pilate went outside again and said to the people, "I am going to bring him out to you now, but understand clearly that I find him not guilty." Then Jesus came out wearing the crown of thorns and the purple robe. And Pilate said, "Look, here is the man!"

When they saw him, the leading priests and Temple guards began shouting, "Crucify him! Crucify him!"

"Take him yourselves and crucify him," Pilate said. "I find him not guilty."

The Jewish leaders replied, "By our law he ought to die because he called himself the Son of God."

#TrustJesus.—When Jesus died on the cross, it wasn't because He committed a sin. Pilate admitted that Jesus was not guilty. Jesus was sinless. Peter would later write, "He committed no sin, neither was deceit found in His mouth." And He remains sinless today. John said, "You know that He appeared in order to take away sins, and in Him, there is no sin." Since we all sin, and the wages of sin is death, Jesus died in our place as our sinless substitute so that our death sentence could be nullified. Right now is the time to believe in Jesus.

Jesus was Sentenced to be Crucified -
John 19:8-16a

When Pilate heard this, he was more frightened than ever. He took Jesus back into the headquarters again and asked him, "Where are you from?" But Jesus gave no answer. "Why don't you talk to me?" Pilate demanded. "Don't you realize that I have the power to release you or crucify you?"

Then Jesus said, "You would have no power over me at all unless it were given to you from above. So the one who handed me over to you has the greater sin."

Then Pilate tried to release him, but the Jewish leaders shouted, "If you release this man, you are no 'friend of Caesar.' Anyone who declares himself a king is a rebel against Caesar."

When they said this, Pilate brought Jesus out to them again. Then Pilate sat down on the judgment seat on the platform that is called the Stone Pavement (in Hebrew, *Gabbatha*). It was now about noon on the day of preparation for the Passover. And Pilate said to the people, "Look, here is your king!"

"Away with him," they yelled. "Away with him! Crucify him!"

"What? Crucify your king?" Pilate asked.

"We have no king but Caesar," the leading priests shouted back.

Then Pilate turned Jesus over to them to be crucified.

#TrustJesus.—Jesus suffered willingly, even when He was tempted to by-pass the cross. Are you grateful that He suffered in your place so that you do not have to suffer punishment for your sins? Not only that, but He died to purchase all things good for you that sin destroyed. Will you trust Jesus today?

Jesus Gave His Life so That You Could Live Forever
- John 19:16b-24

So they took Jesus away. Carrying the cross by himself, he went to the place called Place of the Skull (in Hebrew, *Golgotha*). There they nailed him to the cross. Two others were crucified with him, one on either side, with Jesus between them. And Pilate posted a sign on the cross that read:

JESUS OF NAZARETH, THE KING OF THE JEWS.

The place where Jesus was crucified was near the city, and the sign was written in Hebrew, Latin, and Greek, so that many people could read it.

Then the leading priests objected and said to Pilate, "Change it from 'The King of the Jews' to 'He said, I am King of the Jews.'"

Pilate replied, "No, what I have written, I have written."

When the soldiers had crucified Jesus, they divided his clothes among the four of them. They also took his robe, but it was seamless, woven in one piece from top to bottom. So they said, "Rather than tearing it apart, let's throw dice for it." This fulfilled the Scripture that says, "They divided my garments among themselves and threw dice for my clothing." So that is what they did.

#TrustJesus.—Jesus did not commit one sin while He lived on this earth. God placed your sins and the sins of the whole world, past, present, and future, on Him that day He died on the cross. He did all of this for you. Will you accept Him today?

It is Finished - John 19:25-30

Standing near the cross were Jesus' mother, and his mother's sister, Mary (the wife of Clopas), and Mary Magdalene. When Jesus saw his mother standing there beside the disciple he loved, he said to her, "Dear woman, here is your son." And he said to this disciple, "Here is your mother." And from then on this disciple took her into his home.

Jesus knew that his mission was now finished, and to fulfill Scripture he said, "I am thirsty." A jar of sour wine was sitting there, so they soaked a sponge in it, put it on a hyssop branch, and held it up to his lips. When Jesus had tasted it, he said, "It is finished!" Then he bowed his head and gave up his spirit.

#TrustJesus.—When Jesus said, "It is finished," He was telling you that He paid the debt of sin for the world. Now, you don't have to pay a debt for your sins, because Jesus paid it; and has purchased, with His own blood, a place in Heaven for you, and all who believe in Him. Will you believe in Jesus today?

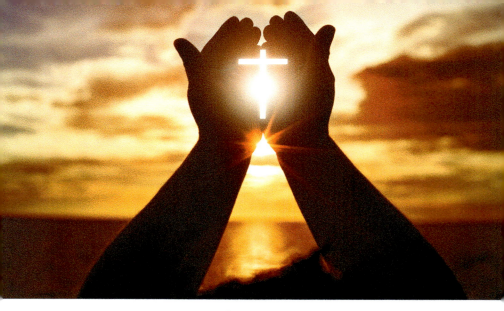

Not a Bone in His Body Was Broken - John 19:31-37

It was the day of preparation, and the Jewish leaders didn't want the bodies hanging there the next day, which was the Sabbath (and a very special Sabbath, because it was Passover week). So they asked Pilate to hasten their deaths by ordering that their legs be broken. Then their bodies could be taken down. So the soldiers came and broke the legs of the two men crucified with Jesus. But when they came to Jesus, they saw that he was already dead, so they didn't break his legs. One of the soldiers, however, pierced his side with a spear, and immediately blood and water flowed out.

(This report is from an eyewitness giving an accurate account. He speaks the truth so that you also may continue to believe.) These things happened in fulfillment of the Scriptures that say, "Not one of his bones will be broken," and "They will look on the one they pierced."

#TrustJesus.—The actions of Jesus on the cross are the center and the pivot for all history. The death, burial and resurrection of the Lord Jesus Christ is the door for salvation for all who call upon His name. Will you call on Him today?

Jesus Was Buried in a Borrowed Tomb - John 19:38-42

Afterward Joseph of Arimathea, who had been a secret disciple of Jesus (because he feared the Jewish leaders), asked Pilate for permission to take down Jesus' body.

When Pilate gave permission, Joseph came and took the body away. With him came Nicodemus, the man who had come to Jesus at night. He brought about seventy-five pounds of perfumed ointment made from myrrh and aloes. Following Jewish burial custom, they wrapped Jesus' body with the spices in long sheets of linen cloth.

The place of crucifixion was near a garden, where there was a new tomb, never used before. And so, because it was the day of preparation for the Jewish Passover and since the tomb was close at hand, they laid Jesus there.

#TrustJesus.—Jesus wants you to know, beyond a shadow of a doubt, who He is! He is no longer in the temporary tomb, but seated at the right hand of God, the Father, in heaven. One day, He will come back to the earth He created and take you home to be with Him for eternity in Heaven. Are you ready?

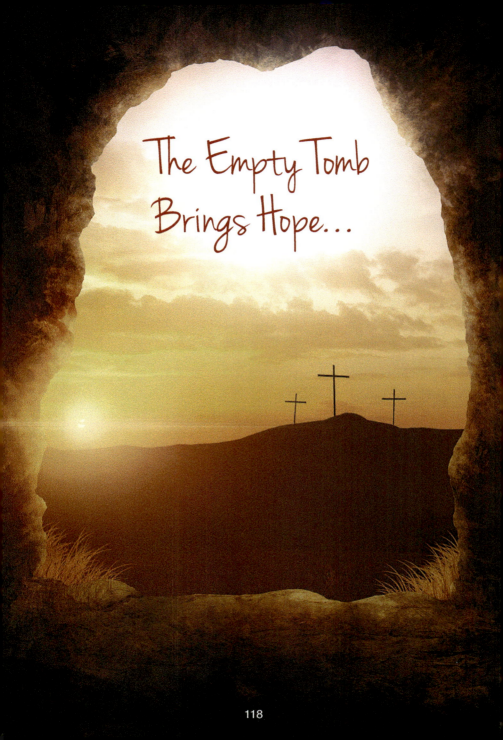

The Empty Tomb Brings Hope...

Jesus Will Empty Your Tomb

The resurrection of the Lord Jesus Christ is the defining difference between Him and any other religious leader. There is an event: the crucifixion and the death. There is a location: the tomb. There is the fact: The Lord Jesus Christ rose from the grave and is alive for evermore as the only way to the Father in heaven.

Peter, John, and Mary Visited the Empty Tomb - John 20:1-10

Early on Sunday morning, while it was still dark, Mary Magdalene came to the tomb and found that the stone had been rolled away from the entrance. She ran and found Simon Peter and the other disciple, the one whom Jesus loved. She said, "They have taken the Lord's body out of the tomb, and we don't know where they have put him!"

Peter and the other disciple started out for the tomb. They were both running, but the other disciple outran Peter and reached the tomb first. He stooped and looked in and saw the linen wrappings lying there, but he didn't go in. Then Simon Peter arrived and went inside. He also noticed the linen wrappings lying there, while the cloth that had covered Jesus' head was folded up and lying apart from the other wrappings.

Then the disciple who had reached the tomb first also went in, and he saw and believed—for until then they still hadn't understood the Scriptures that said Jesus must rise from the dead. Then they went home.

#WalkWithJesus.—The empty tomb proves that Jesus rose from the dead. You are saved by grace because you put your faith in Jesus. This faith is not your own doing, but His gift to you. You cannot boast that you had anything to do with it. Jesus has made you what you are, a new person, created in Him, to serve Him. Do you have the faith to believe that He rose physically from the dead?

Jesus' Angels Gave Hope to Mary. - John 20:11-18

Mary was standing outside the tomb crying, and as she wept, she stooped and looked in. She saw two white-robed angels, one sitting at the head and the other at the foot of the place where the body of Jesus had been lying. "Dear woman, why are you crying?" the angels asked her.

"Because they have taken away my Lord," she replied, "and I don't know where they have put him."

She turned to leave and saw someone standing there. It was Jesus, but she didn't recognize him. "Dear woman, why are you crying?" Jesus asked her. "Who are you looking for?"

She thought he was the gardener. "Sir," she said, "if you have taken him away, tell me where you have put him, and I will go and get him."

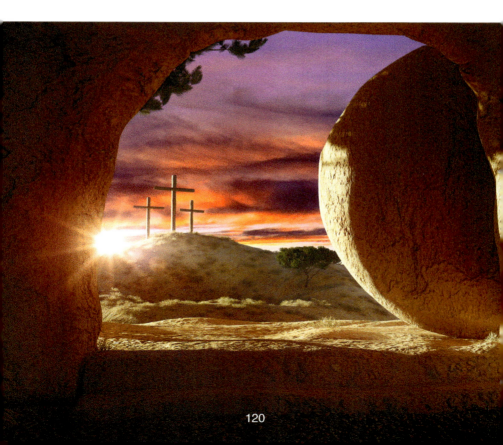

"Mary!" Jesus said.

She turned to him and cried out, "Rabboni!" (which is Hebrew for "Teacher").

"Don't cling to me," Jesus said, "for I haven't yet ascended to the Father. But go find my brothers and tell them, 'I am ascending to my Father and your Father, to my God and your God.'"

Mary Magdalene found the disciples and told them, "I have seen the Lord!" Then she gave them his message.

#WalkWithJesus.—How many times has Jesus come alongside you and you didn't recognize Him? Will you open your spiritual eyes to see His presence?

121

Jesus Appeared to the Disciples, Giving Them Hope - John 20:19-25

That Sunday evening the disciples were meeting behind locked doors because they were afraid of the Jewish leaders. Suddenly, Jesus was standing there among them! "Peace be with you," he said. As he spoke, he showed them the wounds in his hands and his side. They were filled with joy when they saw the Lord! Again he said, "Peace be with you. As the Father has sent me, so I am sending you." Then he breathed on them and said, "Receive the Holy Spirit. If you forgive anyone's sins, they are forgiven. If you do not forgive them, they are not forgiven."

One of the twelve disciples, Thomas (nicknamed the Twin), was not with the others when Jesus came. They told him, "We have seen the Lord!"

But he replied, "I won't believe it unless I see the nail wounds in his hands, put my fingers into them, and place my hand into the wound in his side."

#TrustJesus.—Do not demand, like Thomas, physical assurances to believe in Jesus as your personal Savior. Will you place your complete faith and trust in Him today? He will give you the assurance that your sins are forgiven.

Touching Jesus Brought Hope to the Doubter - John 20:26-31

Eight days later the disciples were together again, and this time Thomas was with them. The doors were locked; but suddenly, as before, Jesus was standing among them. "Peace be with you," he said. Then he said to Thomas, "Put your finger here, and look at my hands. Put your hand into the wound in my side. Don't be faithless any longer. Believe!"

"My Lord and my God!" Thomas exclaimed.

Then Jesus told him, "You believe because you have seen me. Blessed are those who believe without seeing me."

The Purpose of this Book

The disciples saw Jesus do many other miraculous signs in addition to the ones recorded in this book. But these are written so that you may continue to believe that Jesus is the Messiah, the Son of God, and that by believing in him you will have life by the power of his name.

> #TrustJesus.—When Thomas saw Jesus, He acknowledged that He was his Lord and his God. You have not seen Jesus with your physical eyes. You must accept, by saving faith, that He is the Son of God, and by believing you can have eternal life. Will you accept His free gift of eternal life right now?

21

Jesus Appeared on the Lake Shore

Bring Me Some Fish - John 21:1-14

Later, Jesus appeared again to the disciples beside the Sea of Galilee. This is how it happened. Several of the disciples were there—Simon Peter, Thomas (nicknamed the Twin), Nathanael from Cana in Galilee, the sons of Zebedee, and two other disciples.

Simon Peter said, "I'm going fishing."

"We'll come, too," they all said. So they went out in the boat, but they caught nothing all night.

At dawn Jesus was standing on the beach, but the disciples couldn't see who he was. He called out, "Fellows, have you caught any fish?"

"No," they replied.

Then he said, "Throw out your net on the right-hand side of the boat, and you'll get some!" So they did, and they couldn't haul in the net because there were so many fish in it.

Then the disciple Jesus loved said to Peter, "It's the Lord!" When Simon Peter heard that it was the Lord, he put on his tunic (for he had stripped for work), jumped into the water, and headed to shore. The others stayed with the boat and pulled the loaded net to the shore, for they were only about a hundred yards from shore. When they got there, they found breakfast waiting for them—fish cooking over a charcoal fire, and some bread.

"Bring some of the fish you've just caught," Jesus said. So Simon Peter went aboard and dragged the net to the shore. There were 153 large fish, and yet the net hadn't torn.

"Now come and have some breakfast!" Jesus said. None of the disciples dared to ask him, "Who are you?" They knew it was the Lord. Then Jesus served them the bread and the fish. This was the third time Jesus had appeared to his disciples since he had been raised from the dead.

#TrustJesus.—No matter what happens in your life, if Jesus is living in you, you can have the assurance that He is in complete control. The answers might be immediate or they might be in the future. In either case, do not panic, He is in control of your destiny. When you don't understand His ways, trust His Word. When you're not sure what to do next, do the next thing. Will you trust Jesus today?

Jesus Restored Peter's Hope - John 21:15-25

After breakfast Jesus asked Simon Peter, "Simon son of John, do you love me more than these?"

"Yes, Lord," Peter replied, "you know I love you."

"Then feed my lambs," Jesus told him.

Jesus repeated the question: "Simon son of John, do you love me?"

"Yes, Lord," Peter said, "you know I love you."

"Then take care of my sheep," Jesus said.

A third time he asked him, "Simon son of John, do you love me?"

Peter was hurt that Jesus asked the question a third time. He said, "Lord, you know everything. You know that I love you."

Jesus said, "Then feed my sheep.

"I tell you the truth, when you were young, you were able to do as you liked; you dressed yourself and went wherever you wanted to go. But when you are old, you will stretch out your hands, and others will dress you and take you where you don't want to go." Jesus said this to let him know by what kind of death he would glorify God. Then Jesus told him, "Follow me."

Peter turned around and saw behind them the disciple Jesus loved—the one who had leaned over to Jesus during supper and asked, "Lord, who will betray you?" Peter asked Jesus, "What about him, Lord?"

Jesus replied, "If I want him to remain alive until I return, what is that to you? As for you, follow me." So the rumor spread among the community of believers that this disciple wouldn't die. But that isn't what Jesus said at all. He only said, "If I want him to remain alive until I return, what is that to you?"

This disciple is the one who testifies to these events and has recorded them here. And we know that his account of these things is accurate.

Jesus also did many other things. If they were all written down, I suppose the whole world could not contain the books that would be written.

#LoveJesus.—"Dear friends, let us continue to love one another, for love comes from God. Anyone who loves is a child of God and knows God. But anyone who does not love does not know God, for God is love. God showed how much he loved us by sending his one and only Son into the world so that we might have eternal life through him. This is real love—not that we loved God, but that he loved us and sent his Son as a sacrifice to take away our sins."

Epilogue

Jesus is in the Best Place to Help You

Jesus Ascended Into Heaven - Luke 24:44-53

He said to them, "This is what I told you while I was still with you: Everything must be fulfilled that is written about me in the Law of Moses, the Prophets and the Psalms."

Then he opened their minds so they could understand the Scriptures. He told them, "This is what is written: The Messiah will suffer and rise from the dead on the third day, and repentance for the forgiveness of sins will be preached in his name to all nations, beginning at Jerusalem. You are witnesses of these things. I am going to send you what my Father has promised; but stay in the city until you have been clothed with power from on high."

When he had led them out to the vicinity of Bethany, he lifted up his hands and blessed them. While he was blessing them, he left them and was taken up into heaven. Then they worshiped him and returned to Jerusalem with great joy. And they stayed continually at the temple, praising God.

#TrustJesus.—The same way Jesus ascended into Heaven, He will one day come back to take you where He lives. He wants you to live with Him in heaven for all eternity. Now there is only one question that is of interest to God and you. That question is, "Will you accept Jesus today as your personal Savior?" You are saved by grace because you put your faith in Him. It is not your own doing, but His gift to you.

Do You Know That You Will Live Forever With Jesus in Heaven?

More than two thousand years ago, God sent Jesus into the world He created. He became one of you, but He did nothing wrong. He showed the world what God is like – loving, merciful and kind. He healed the sick people; the blind were made to see, the deaf to hear, and the lame to walk. Some people followed Him, and He gave them a new way of life —God's way. But others hated Him because He was so good, and He exposed their evil ways.

This is what He did for you

"God loved everyone in the world so much that He gave Jesus, His One and only Son, to die for each of them. Now everyone who believes in Him will not perish, but will have eternal life. For God did not send Him to bring punishment to the people of the world, but that they might be saved through believing in Him" (John 3:16,17).

Jesus is perfect and wants to be your friend. But, when you do not obey Him, then that is called sin. The penalty for sin is death. He lived a perfect life and gave Himself as a sacrifice, a payment for your sins. He did all this because He loves you. His death on the cross frees you from your sin and brings you into friendship with God, the Father.

Three days after Jesus died, He came back from the dead and is alive! Now everyone who believes in Him will not perish but will have eternal life. He will forgive your sins, be your Savior, and meet your needs. He is the only one who can do this for you.

He will free you from your guilt and shame and give you a new life. He will heal your brokenness and make you whole. He will teach you how to live a life that honors God, the Father.

If you put your faith and trust in Him, you can stop living by everyone else's rules, and you can start living by the principles He has given you in the Bible. He loves you more than anyone else because He created you for a purpose. He wants you, more than anything, to follow Him let Him direct your path in life.

Now, Are You Ready and Willing to...

- Trust in Jesus completely for eternal life, knowing that you cannot save yourself?

- Believe that He took your place, and paid for all your sins on the cross?

- Repent of your sins and follow Him?

- Receive God's gift of eternal life through Jesus?

If you can answer YES to these questions, then you are ready to pray the following prayer, believing it in your heart. Will you pray now to make Jesus your Savior and your friend?

Pray this prayer and believe it in your heart

Dear Jesus, I confess that I have sinned and cannot save myself. I believe that You died for me. Please forgive me of my sin and come into my heart right now and save me. Help me to turn from my sin and become Your follower. Amen.

We are so Glad You Prayed the Prayer!

The Christian life is, by far, the most joy-filled life that any person could ever live. Jesus wants you to know that there is joy in Heaven because of your decision to receive Him as your Savior.

It was by faith that you accepted God's free gift of eternal life, and now, by faith, you must believe that God will do all He said He would do. There are two important truths that He wants you to know about your eternal life.

God cannot lie. This truth gives you confidence that you have eternal life, which God, Who cannot lie, promised before the world was created. If God Father makes a promise to you, it will come to pass.

God's Word is sure. "I have written this to you who believe in the name of the Son of God, so that you may know you have eternal life. And we are confident that He hears us whenever we ask for anything that pleases Him. And since we know He hears us when we make our requests, we also know that He will give us what we ask for" (1 John 5:13-15).

Don't be surprised at the things Jesus will do in your life as you begin to follow Him in your Christian life. He will be there for you in your newfound faith, and He will help you overcome temptations in your life.

There will be times when you don't know what to do and which way to turn. By reading His Word, and relying on Him to guide you through life, you will know the plan He has for you. The best thing you can do for Him right now is to find another Christian believer to celebrate with. This is the first day of the rest of your life on earth, and you have eternity with Jesus to look forward too. Now, tell someone else about it.

Get to Know Believers Like You in His Church

As you continue your walk as a new believer in Jesus, you need to meet with other believers just like you. In his local church, you will find more of His followers who will pray for you and guide you as you learn to live for Him with all your heart.

Reach Up to God —Reach Out to Others

In this book you have discovered that Jesus alone brings healing, wholeness, and transformation. Jesus is the Way, the Truth, and the Life. Jesus brings hope; Hope that He is listening. Hope that He cares. Hope that brings a vision of a better tomorrow and a future that awaits you in Heaven.

Now, share this book with your family and friends. You can instantly download the ebook version of *I Am Jesus: The Giver of Hope* by scanning the QR Code below.

SCAN ME